BASIC WING CHUN TRAINING

WING CHUN KUNG FU TRAINING FOR STREET FIGHTING AND SELF-DEFENSE

SAM FURY

Illustrated by
NEIL GERMIO

WARNINGS AND DISCLAIMERS

CONTENTS

THANKS FOR YOUR PURCHASE

Did you know you can get FREE chapters of any SF Nonfiction Book you want?

https://offers.SFNonfictionBooks.com/Free-Chapters

You will also be among the first to know of FREE review copies, discount offers, bonus content, and more.

Go to:

https://offers.SFNonfictionBooks.com/Free-Chapters

Thanks again for your support.

INTRODUCTION

I wrote this book as a progressive training guide to teach those interested in Wing Chun the fundamental techniques and concepts, and how they can be applied to modern street-fighting scenarios.

Although I feel anyone with an interest in martial arts will gain value from it, it's primarily intended for:

- People who are thinking about learning Wing Chun, but first want insight.
- People who want some basic knowledge of principles and techniques before joining a Wing Chun class.
- Beginners who are already learning Wing Chun and want to supplement their training.
- Teachers of Wing Chun who want some ideas for training beginner students.
- Anyone that wants to self-train in Wing Chun kung fu.

In any case, whoever you are and for whatever reason you purchased this book, I sincerely hope that you get some value from it.

GETTING THE MOST FROM THIS BOOK

To get the most out of this book, you should practice the exercises regularly. A training schedule is included in the book bonuses; I recommend that you follow it.

Practice all the exercises slowly to begin with. Get the techniques right and learn to understand the static movements first, then build your speed and power. Practice all exercises on both sides of your body.

All the lessons in this book focus purely on the adaptation of Wing Chun. It is advised that you also have a physical fitness regime. See www.SurvivalFitnessPlan.com for detailed coverage of physical fitness training.

One of the big differences between this and other Wing Chun training books is that this book shows how to adapt Wing Chun lessons to a modern street fight. In a real fight, you won't be up against another Wing Chun practitioner. When you're training, it's important that your training partner doesn't attack you like a Wing Chun fighter. Most people will fight like boxers/Muay Thai fighters, so many of the exercises are adapted to defending against common attacks in those styles.

In a real street fight, you probably won't have the chance to get into your Wing Chun stance, and even if you do, it's not advisable. You do not want to let your opponent know what you're going to do. Instead, move freely and naturally, not rigidly. Once you're in Wing Chun fighting range you can use the appropriate principles and techniques.

Keep an open mind and adapt what you learn in a way that works for you. There are no restrictions, and you don't know how your opponent is going to react. The exercises are merely examples of what could be done. Since this book adapts Wing Chun to modern street fighting, many of the exercises included may not be considered traditional, or may be known by different names.

When training, do things properly. Put feeling and movement into the techniques. If your execution is sloppy and weak when you train, that's how it will be in reality. If you do the exercises properly, it will ingrain the correct muscle memory so that you'll still be able to react properly in times of stress. You'll hit your opponent correctly and apply pressure in the right places. Your body will have the correct posture and placement, and you'll instinctively know where your opponent is.

Although you train for reality, it's still training. There will be many times when you're practicing with your partner that you may think, "But I can just hit him/her here" or "I could easily block that." These things may be true, and it's good to think of them, but you are learning. Give each other the time to learn. Understand the principles and do the exercises properly. You can express yourself fully during free sparring.

Use training equipment. You want to be able to train hard, but you do not want to get injured. The only way to do this is to use proper training equipment, such as pads and sparring equipment.

Even when using training equipment, you will still feel pain sometimes. It's good to be conditioned to pain. In a real fight you will feel pain, and your body will react differently when it does so. It's useful to be aware of that. Start gently and gradually increase force to build your pain tolerance.

LESSON 1: THE HALF SQUAT

This shoulder-width half squat will help you build the leg muscles needed for many of the following exercises.

It's important to build strength in this way, as it will help with balance, footwork, stepping, turning, and many other things.

Stand straight with your feet together and your hands by your sides, then bend your knees slightly and turn your heels out.

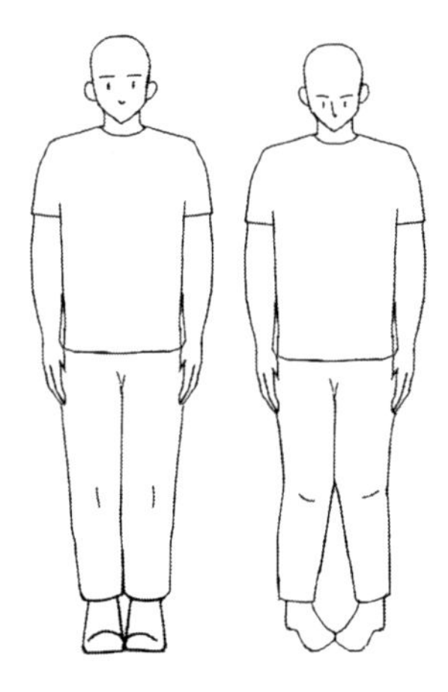

Plant your heels down and turn your toes out, then plant your toes and turn your heels out. Make fists and bring them in under your chest, on either side of your torso.

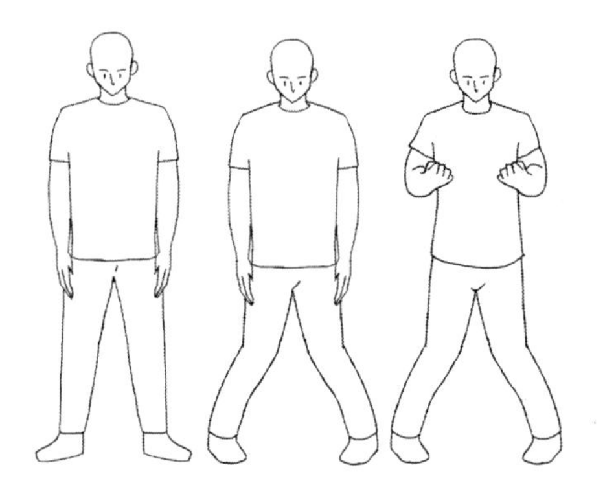

Remember these five steps to get to this position. This will be referred to as the half squat position, and is the starting point for some exercises.

While in this position, drop your knees down and then come back up. This is one squat.

Your knees should never fully straighten.

Exercise 1: The Half Squat

Do as many half squats as you can in a given period.

LESSON 2: FIGHTING STANCE

In a real fight, you probably won't adopt this exact fighting stance, but it's good for facilitating the correct application of techniques when you're learning, and is often used as a starting position for upcoming exercises.

Lead and Rear Sides

Whichever leg and hand are forward-most are your leads. Whichever leg and hand are to the back is your rear.

In actual combat, your strongest side will preferably be your lead, but you should always train on both sides.

Adopting the Fighting Stance

Start in the half squat. While keeping your feet in the same spot, turn on them so that one leg is in front of the other.

Put your hands up to around chest height. If your right (or left) leg is forward-most, your right (or left) hand should be as well.

Your rear leg should support approximately 70% of your body weight. You should be able to easily lift your lead foot into the air if needed—to kick, for example. Keep your arms slightly bent.

Switching Sides

Learning the correct way to switch sides helps to build strength in the legs, gets you familiar with how to turn your body, and encourages correct weight distribution, which helps with stability and increasing the power of your strikes.

Start in the fighting stance.

Assuming you are in a left lead stance, rotate your body with your feet to the right. You will rotate 180°.

As you do so, your body weight will shift from your left leg to your right, and your hands will also change position.

You'll finish in the fighting stance, with a right lead.

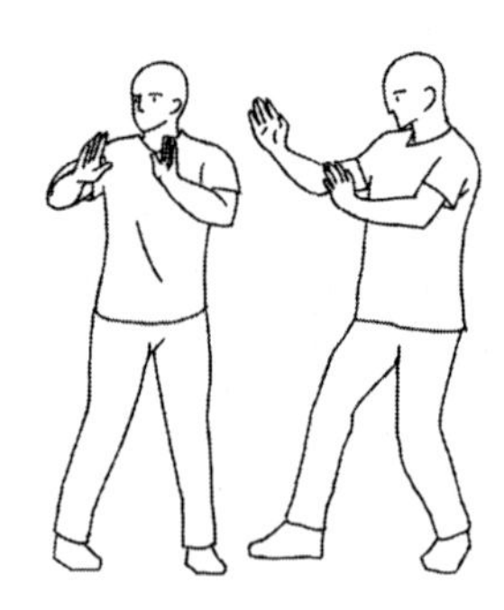

Exercise 2: Switching Sides

Repeat the switching sides exercise from left to right and vice versa.

Related Chapters:

- Lesson 1: The Half Squat

LESSON 3: BASIC FOOTWORK

Correct footwork is very important. Without it, you'll become unbalanced, and your techniques will lose effectiveness.

The primary use of footwork is to control distance. Knowing when and how to close or gain distance allows you to effectively attack and defend. You want to be able to attack, but not get hit. When your opponent moves back, you can move forward, and vice versa. There is no need to rush in all the time. Be smart. Always consider distance.

Stepping Forward

The amount you step forward will depend on the distance you want to cover. The shorter the distance, the more stable you will be. A half step is good for practice.

From the fighting stance, step forward with your lead leg about half a step. Put weight on your lead leg and slide your rear leg up.

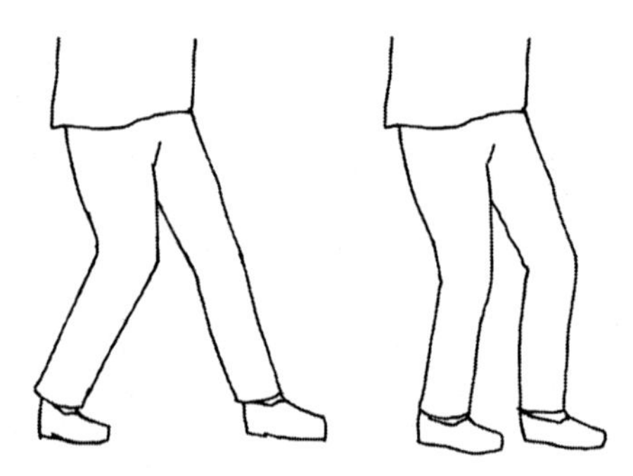

Put weight back on your rear leg and step forward with your lead foot again.

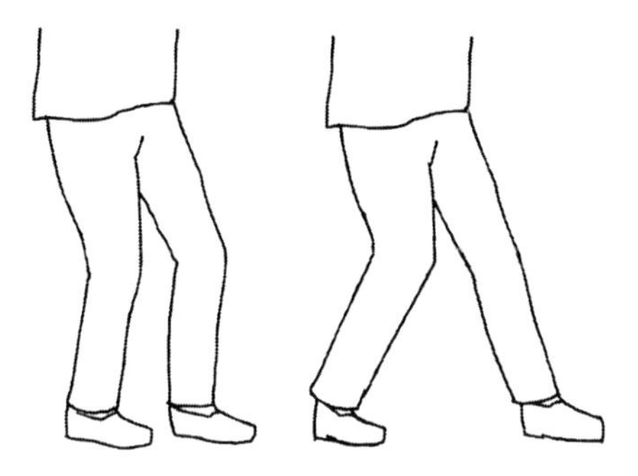

Repeat this for a number of steps.

Switch sides to turn around. Ensure you also change your lead hand.

Exercise 3: Stepping Forward

Practice stepping forward for a given distance, such as the length of your training area.

Use the switching sides movement to change your lead side and then practice stepping forward on this new side.

When you're ready, increase the speed of your steps.

Moving Backwards

To move backwards, just do the opposite of what you did when stepping forward. That is, move your rear foot first.

Exercise 4: Stepping Forwards and Backwards

Step forward a few times and then step backward. Practice doing this on both sides.

Stepping Through

This is a way you can step forward and switch sides at the same time. This lesson also contains a way to get behind your opponent using a variation of this movement.

From the fighting stance, slide your rear foot up and curve it in slightly towards your lead. At the same time, bring your rear hand through to become the new lead.

Move your rear foot past your current and then curve it out slightly to place it in the new lead position. Move your hands and feet together to move forward and adopt the new lead side.

Exercise 5: Stepping Through

Practice the stepping through movement. Increase your speed when you're ready.

Stepping Though Application

This demonstrates how you can use a slight variation of the stepping-through technique to get behind your opponent.

When practicing techniques for practical use, it's important to begin from a natural stance, since that's a more realistic scenario.

As your opponent strikes, move your leads to the outside of his/her body and deflect his/her arm at the same time. Do not step straight in. You will get hit.

Move your lead foot forward, behind your opponent, and then pivot on your lead until you're facing his/her back.

Once you're at your opponent's back, you can attack.

Here it is from the opposite side.

Exercise 6: Stepping Behind Your Opponent

Practice using this variation of the stepping-through movement to get behind your opponent. Don't worry about attacking. Focus on your footwork

Related Chapters:

- Lesson 2: Fighting Stance

LESSON 4: SINGLE PUNCH

Learning correct technique for throwing a single punch introduces many important Wing Chun concepts, including body alignment, weight distribution, the changing of hands, correct striking technique, and balance.

Changing Hands

Your starting position for this exercise is with your legs in the half squat position and your hands up, as in the fighting position.

From this neutral position, begin to change your lead hand.

As you do so, shift most of your body weight (approximately 70%) onto the same side as your new lead hand. Your body should tilt in such a way that your eye is in line with your lead hand. Switch lead hands from right to left.

Exercise 7: Changing Hands

Practice changing hands from left to right.

Single Punch

This builds on the previous exercise, with the incorporation of a single punch.

When striking your limb should never become fully straightened. This is true for punches and kicks. Not only is the shock bad for your elbows and knees, you will also be more likely to miss.

Start in the half squat position, with your hands up and your arms relaxed.

Punch out with your lead hand. As you do so, tilt your body and turn slightly, so most of your weight is on your rear leg. Your rear hand is your guard.

Notice the line of your body. You are angling out but punching to the center. Shifting your weight generates power and also places you out of your opponent's attack line.

After you punch, open your hand to relax it. Do not start or stay stiff when you strike. You will lose power and speed. As you relax your punching hand, begin to punch with your other hand. Shift your weight to your other leg.

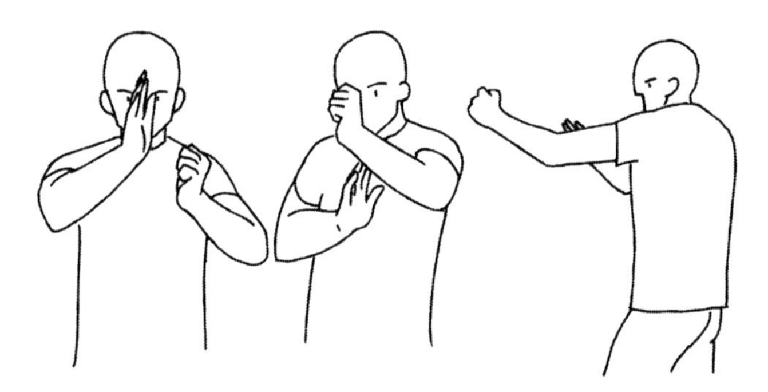

Do not overextend your arm. Your elbow should never lock.

Exercise 8: Single Punch

Practice the single punch from left to right.

Related Chapters:

- Lesson 1: The Half Squat

LESSON 5: TRIPLE PUNCH

Throwing multiple punches in quick succession will result in a loss of power, but can be very useful in an actual fight. Practicing the triple punch will help you to develop the muscle memory needed for repeating punches.

Begin in the half squat position, with your hands up. Punch straight out in front of you and then relax your hand by opening it. Do not shift your weight as much as you did during the single punch exercise.

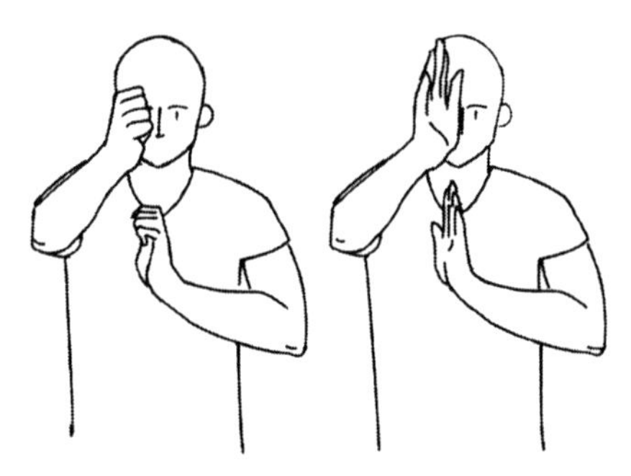

As you bring the hand back in, punch with your other hand.

Relax your hand and punch with your other hand.

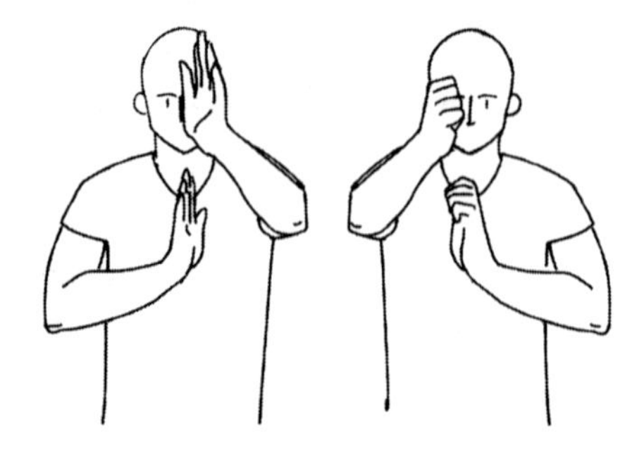

This makes a set of three punches.

Every time you punch, open your hand.

Do another set, but start with the opposite hand. If you did the first punch with your right hand in the first set, then do it with your left hand in the second set.

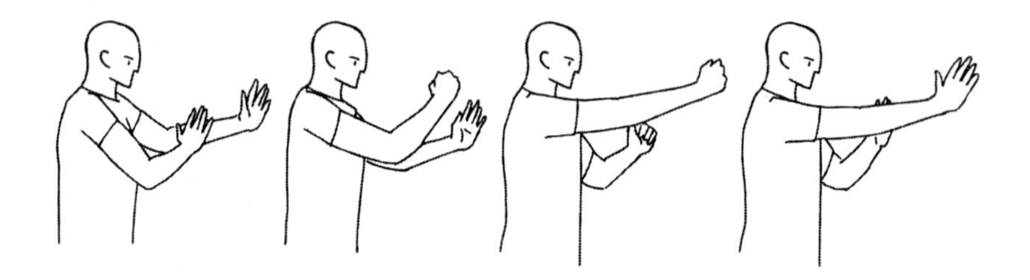

Exercise 9: Triple Punch

Practice the triple punch. Start slowly and remember to relax your hand after each punch. Increase your speed when you're ready.

Related Chapters:

- Lesson 1: The Half Squat
- Lesson 4: Single Punch

LESSON 6: STEPPING PUNCH

Combining stepping forward with a single punch allows you to close distance while attacking. The important lesson of using your body to generate power is emphasized.

Start in the fighting stance. As you move forward, punch with your lead hand. Your whole body should move at once.

When you complete the punch, relax (be ready to defend if needed), then do another one.

Exercise 10: Stepping Punch

Practice the stepping punch. When you're ready, use switching sides to change your lead leg and then practice on your other side.

Exercise 11: Stepping Punch and Stepping Backward

Use the stepping punch to move forward and stepping backward to return to your original spot. Practice on both sides of your body.

Related Chapters:

- Lesson 2: Fighting Stance
- Lesson 4: Single Punch

LESSON 7: TAN SAU

This lesson teaches the basic application of Tan Sau (dispersing hand), a Wing Chun arm and hand position primarily used as a defensive technique. It emphasizes the use of the body to do the work, as opposed to just the hand. It also introduces grabbing, the counterattack, and the concept of telegraphing.

Wing Chun defense is designed to deflect attacks as opposed to defeating them through direct force. This allows the weaker person to gain some leverage over a stronger opponent.

Tan Sau is a good way to deal with mid-level straight attacks. Begin in the half squat position, with your hands up.

Move your palm up and out from your center. Your elbow should end up about a fist-and-a-half's length away from your body.

Turn your whole body to the side. Your hand and body should turn together, and your waist should the work, not your arm. Keep your other hand to the inside and ready for defense.

Relax your lead hand into the normal fighting stance position and then swap your lead hand.

Turn to your other side using a combination of switching sides and Tan Sau. Notice that you don't turn fully to the opposite side. It's closer to half the movement of the switching sides exercise. Relax your hand and repeat the process.

Exercise 12: Tan Sau

Practice using Tan Sau in this manner, from left to right.

Tan Sau Application

This demonstrates the application of Tan Sau. It helps you to learn where to put your hand to defend against a real attack.

As your opponent punches, use Tan Sau to deflect the attack.

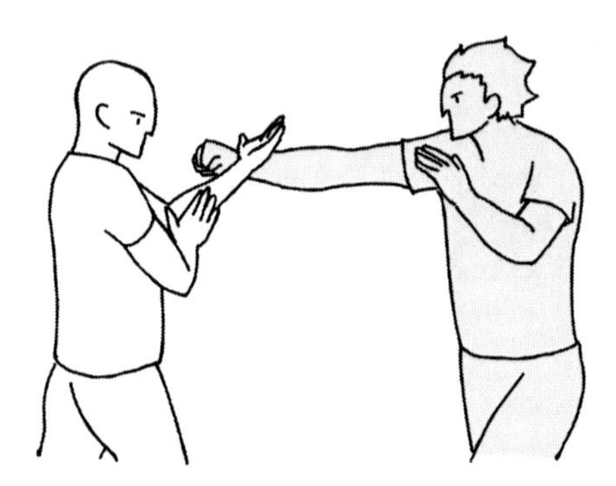

The previous exercise was an exaggerated movement. Adapt what you learn to new situations. Continue to shift your body weight, but only as much as needed.

Your hand should not go out any further than needed to push the punch past your body. This is true with all Wing Chun defensive movements, and is in line with the economy of motion principle, which is that you should only move as much as needed.

You still use your whole body to turn and keep your rear hand to the inside.

Repeat this movement, turning left and right.

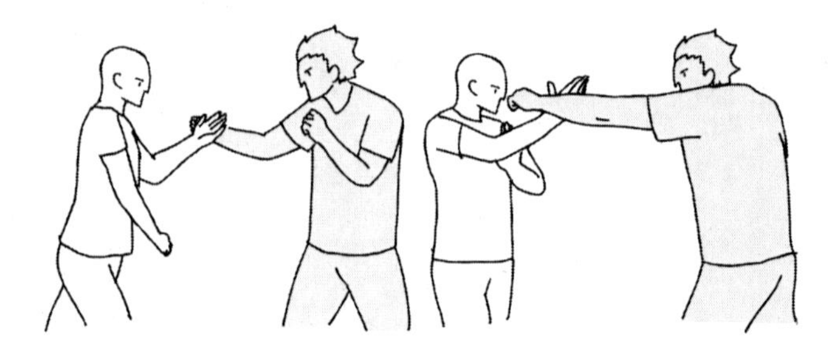

Exercise 13: Tan Sau Application

Practice using Tan Sau to deflect an incoming attack. Practice on both sides of your body.

Related Chapters:

- Lesson 1: The Half Squat
- Lesson 2: Fighting Stance
- Lesson 8: Counterattack
- Lesson 9: Grabbing

LESSON 8: COUNTERATTACK

A counterattack, also referred to as countering, is an attack made in response to another attack.

As your opponent strikes, use Tan Sau to defend. Use the same hand to attack your opponent's eye.

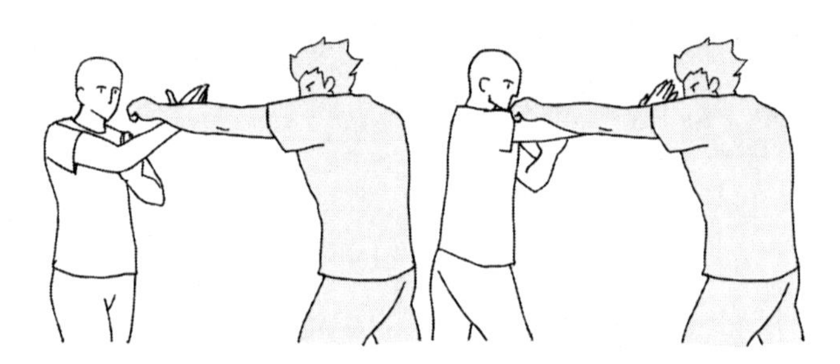

When your hand and body are in the right position, you will be in line to strike.When striking, never retract your limb as it will telegraph your intention—that is, it will let your opponent know what you are about to do.

Never punch an opponent's face. There are too many bones in the face, and you'll hurt your hand. If your hand gets hurt, you won't be effective in grabbing, punching, etc.

In training, punch the body and in a real fight, punch your opponent's body or throat. If you want to hit his/her face, use an open hand, elbow, or knee, and stay away from his/her teeth.

Exercise 14: Tan Sau Counter

Practice this Tan Sau and counterattack movement.

Related Chapters:

- Lesson 7: Tan Sau

LESSON 9: GRABBING

Grabbing your opponent allows you to have greater control over him/her.

When he/she strikes, use Tan Sau to deflect.

As soon as your Tan Sau connects with your opponent, bring your other hand underneath his/her arm and grab it from the outside.

Now you can strike with your hand—by giving your opponent a chop to the throat or attacking his/her eyes, for example—or perhaps use your leg.

If your weight distribution is incorrect, you won't be able to kick or move freely.

Exercise 15: Grabbing

Practice grabbing the hand and countering. Don't worry about kicking yet. You'll learn that soon.

Related Chapters:

- Lesson 7: Tan Sau

LESSON 10: PAK SAU

Pak Sau (slapping hand) is another fundamental Wing Chun movement. This lesson demonstrates using Pak Sau as a defensive technique. It also emphasizes awareness of body positioning, grabbing, and turning from one side to the other.

As the punch comes in, turn your body to the side and press the side of your palm (below your little finger) into your opponent's elbow. Your hand should come directly out from the center of your body. Use your whole body in the movement. You want to hurt your opponent at the same time.

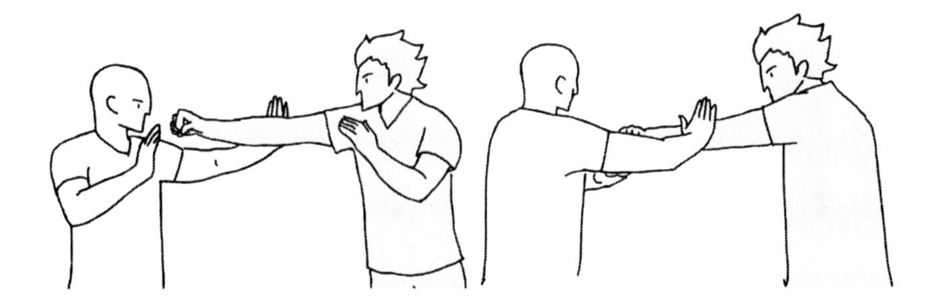

It is important to turn your body to the side, or you'll get hit.

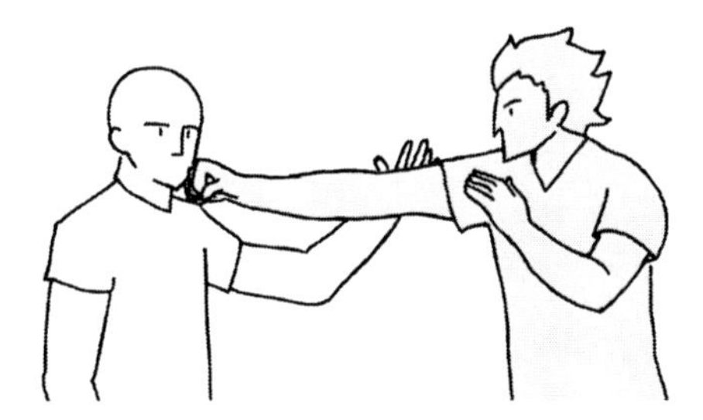

Exercise 16: Pak Sau

Practice using Pak Sau in this manner, from left to right and vice versa.

Pak Sau Counter

After using Pak Sau, you can counter with a direct strike to the face, such as a finger strike to your opponent's eyes.

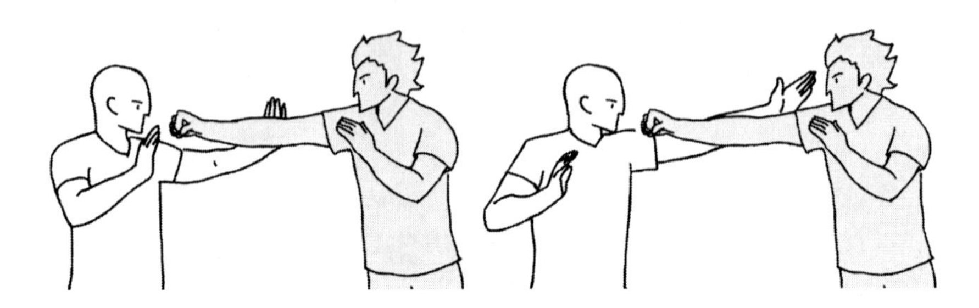

Exercise 17: Pak Sau Counter

Practice countering after using Pak Sau.

Pak Sau Grab Counter

After you defend, you can use your other hand to grab and then counter. Bring up your other hand and grab your opponent's wrist. As you grab his/her wrist, turn it a little bit. At the same time, either strike or apply pressure to the elbow.

Exercise 18: Pak Sau Grab Counter

Practice this defend, grab, and counterattack maneuver.

If your opponent brings up his/her other hand to defend him-/herself, grab it and turn him/her. Now you can attack on this side.

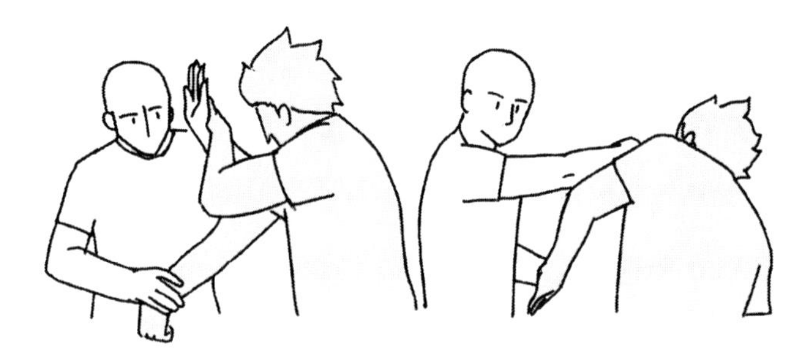

Exercise 19: Pak Sau Grab Counter Extended

Add this second grab and attack to the previous exercise.

Related Chapters:

- Lesson 8: Counterattack
- Lesson 9: Grabbing

LESSON 11: DEFENDING AGAINST THE HOOK-CROSS COMBINATION

This demonstrates how you can use Tan Sau and Pak Sau to defend against a common boxing combination. It's just one of many ways in which Tan Sau and Pak Sau can work together.

As your opponent throws a hook punch at you, use Tan Sau to defend against it.

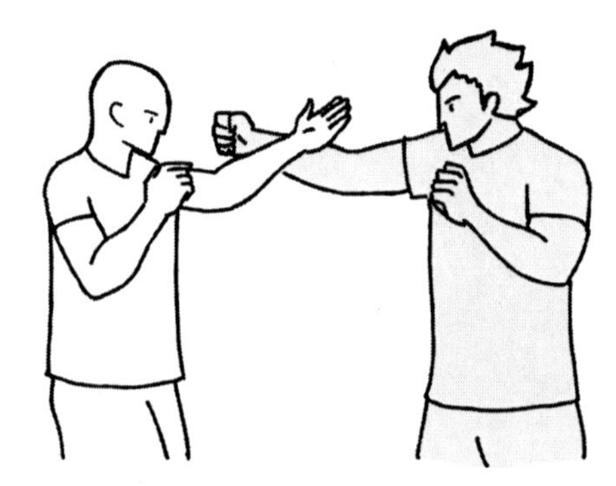

As he/she follows up with a cross, step back and use Pak Sau to deflect it.

Remember to turn your whole body when making the movements and to keep your other hand in to guard your centerline (lesson 12).

Exercise 20: Hook Cross Defense

Practice using Tan Sau and Pak Sau to defend against the hook-cross combination.

Related Chapters:

- Lesson 7: Tan Sau
- Lesson 10: Pak Sau

LESSON 12: CENTERLINE PRINCIPLE

The centerline principle is a core concept in Wing Chun kung fu. Most, if not all, of the exercises in this book are focused on protecting your own centerline while controlling your opponent's.

Your centerline is an imaginary line drawn vertically down the center of your body. All the vital organs are located near the center of the body. Keep it away from your opponent by angling it away from him/her.

Controlling the position of your centerline in relation to your opponent's is done with footwork. Understanding the centerline will allow you to instinctively know where your opponent is.

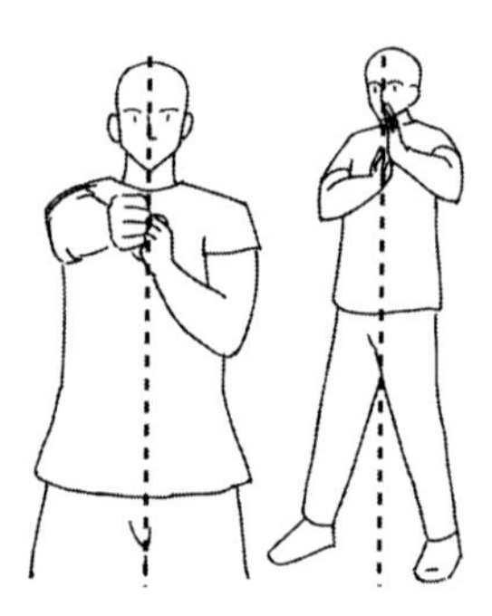

Your central line (different from your centerline) is drawn from your angled center to your opponent.

Offensively, you generate the most power when punching out from your center, since you can incorporate your whole body and hips.

When you're attacking in a straight line, your centerline should face away from your opponent, while your central line faces his/her center.

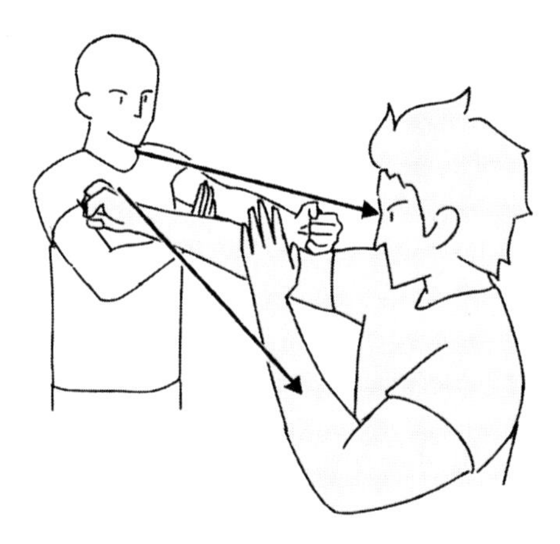

With hook punches and other circular attacks, the center- and central lines merge.

There are three main guidelines for the centerline.

- The one who controls the centerline will control the fight.
- Protect and maintain your own centerline while you control and exploit your opponent's.
- Control the centerline by occupying it.

Direct Line Punching

The following simple exercise demonstrates a number of fundamental principles in Wing Chun Kung Fu. Controlling the centerline, using attack and defense at the same time, and attacking in a direct line.

As your opponent punches, move to the outside of his/her guard. Use a straight punch to deflect the strike and attack at the same time. Your arm should be against his/her elbow. Take special note of your body alignment. Follow up with a second punch to the ribs.

Exercise 21: Direct Line Punching

Practice the direct line punching described.

LESSON 13: BONG SAU

Bong Sau (wing arm) is a defensive technique unique to Wing Chun. It's used to divert a punch by creating an angle of deflection.

Begin in the half squat position, with your hands up. In one movement, turn your hand down and your elbow up. As you do so, turn your waist and tilt your body so your feet are in a fighting stance. Your waist should do the work, not your arm.

Keep your arm in line. You other hand is a guard hand in case your opponent's strike passes through.

This is Bong Sau.

Turn slightly back and bring your hand back to the center.

Switch hand positions so your other hand becomes your lead. Shift your weight to match your new position and then do Bong Sau on your other side.

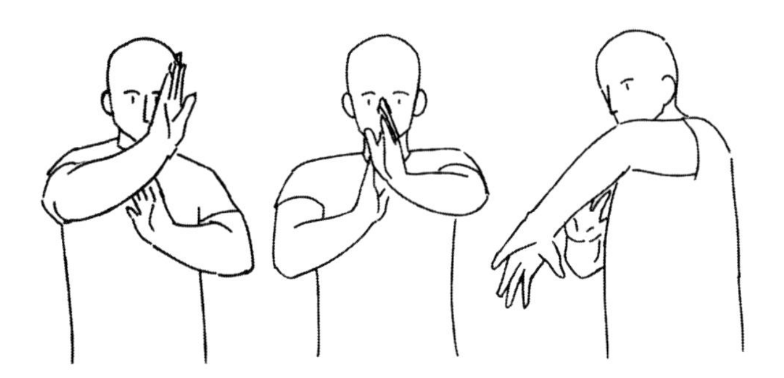

Exercise 22: Bong Sau

Practice Bong Sau from left to right and vice versa.

Bong Sau Strike

This adds a strike to the Bong Sau.

Do Bong Sau as previously described. Shift your body back to center. As you do so, bring your arm up towards your face. Your palm should end up in front of you as if you're reading something off it. You should keep your other hand in the rear as a guard.

Strike out with your lead. Ensure you use the body weight shift as you did in the single punch exercise. Strike with your whole body, and as you bring your hand back, go into Bong Sau on your other side.

Do the strike on this new side.

There are three separate movements to do on each side, and each movement uses the whole body.

1. Bong Sau
2. Return
3. Strike

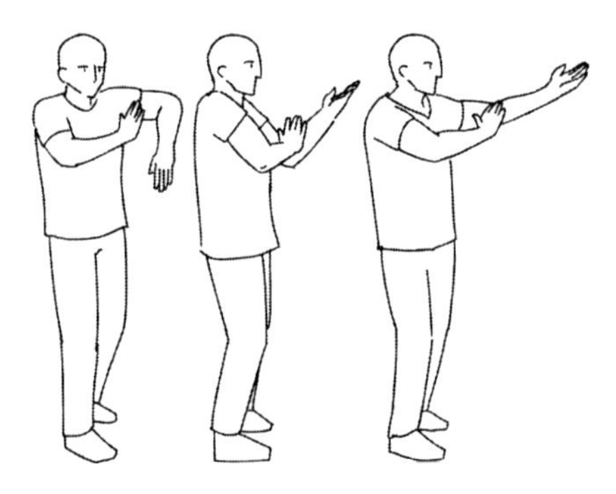

Exercise 23: Bong Sau Strike

Practice doing Bong Sau with the strike.

Related Chapters:

- Lesson 1: The Half Squat
- Lesson 2: Fighting Stance
- Lesson 4: Single Punch

LESSON 14: LAP SAU DRILL

The Lap Sau (pulling hand) drill is a basic Wing Chun drill which teaches you about grabbing and pulling, among other things.

It's important to remember that this is a training drill. You need to work together to make it work. It's not about beating your partner, but about understanding the flow of energy between you.

Begin in Bong Sau and have your partner place his/her arm on top of yours. Grab each other's wrists. It is important that your elbows be locked together.

Pull down your opponent's arm by the hand.

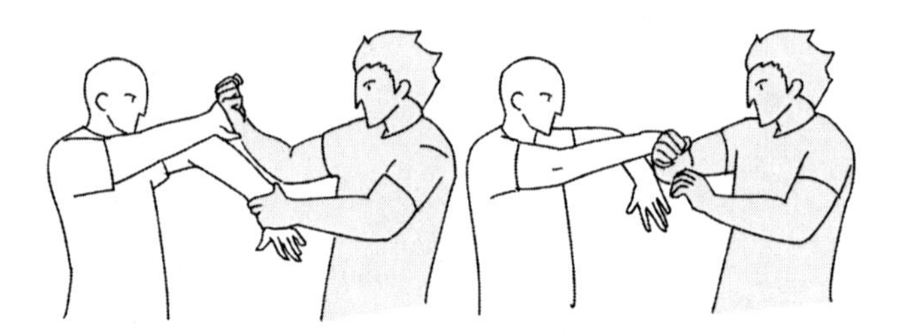

At the same time, rotate your other arm up. Your partner brings his/her hand up to grab your arm.

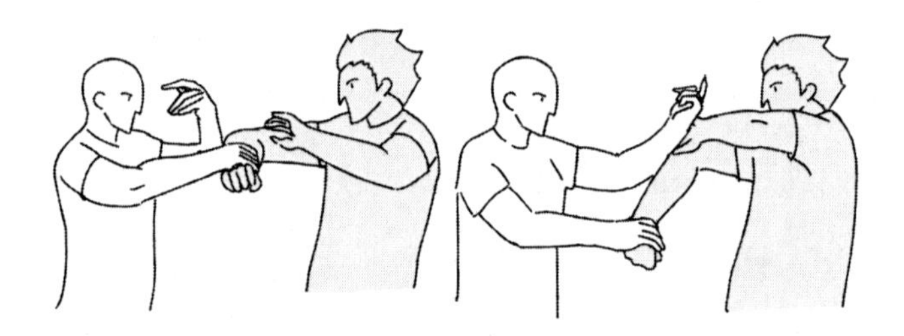

Then he/she pulls your arm down. Repeat this process.

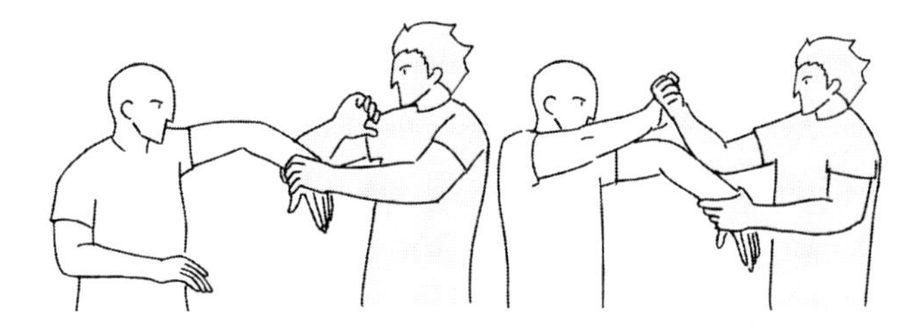

To know if your Bong Sau is correct, try to palm your partner. If your arm isn't firm, or is too straight, he/she will be able to hit you. If your arm is firm and in the correct position, your partner's hand will be deflected above your head.

If your partner holds on to your wrist while you pull, the action will break his/her hold.

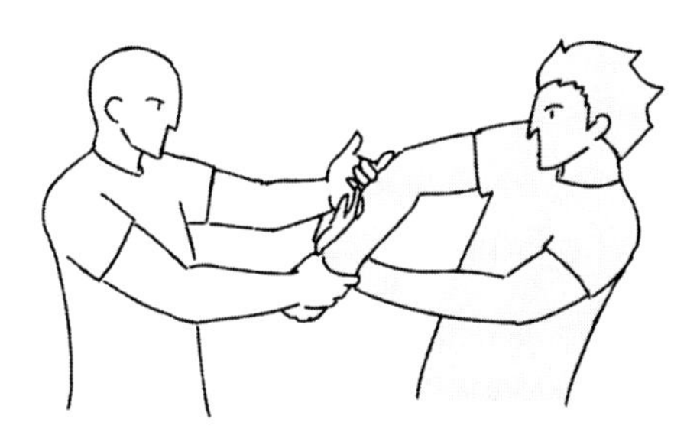

Exercise 24: Lap Sau

Practice the Lap Sau drill on both sides.

Lap Sau Change

Once you're comfortable with Lap Sau on each side, you can learn to change sides in a flowing manner. As your partner comes to grab your hand, turn your wrist, and grab his/hers.

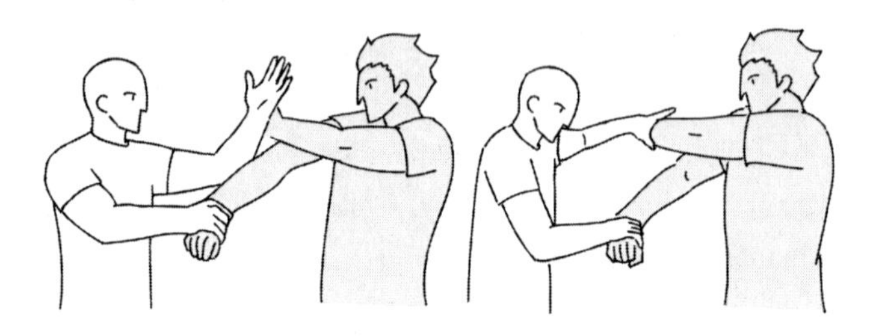

Pull his/her arm down and place your Bong Sau on top. While you do this, change your lead leg to match.

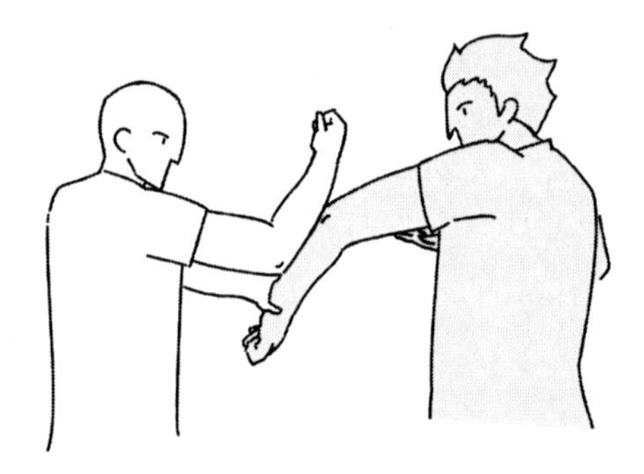

Continue with the Lap Sau drill on this new side.

Exercise 25: Lap Sau Change

Practice changing sides while doing the Lap Sau drill.

Lap Sau Arm Lock

The Lap Sau can be applied to real fighting scenarios in many ways.

Grab your opponent's arm and twist it down as you would in the Lap Sau drill, with your other arm on top.

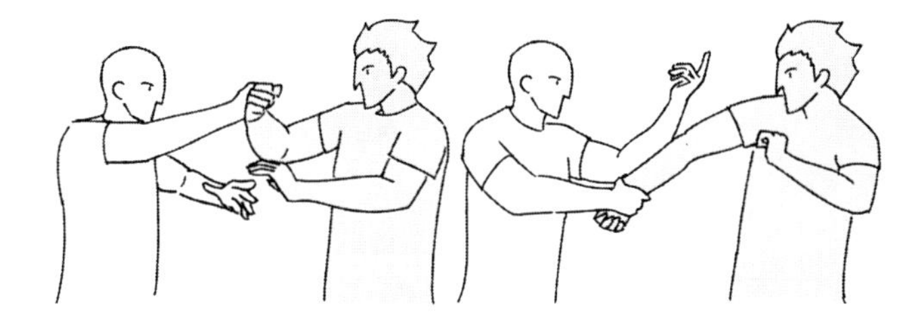

Apply pressure onto your opponent's elbow to perform a basic arm lock.

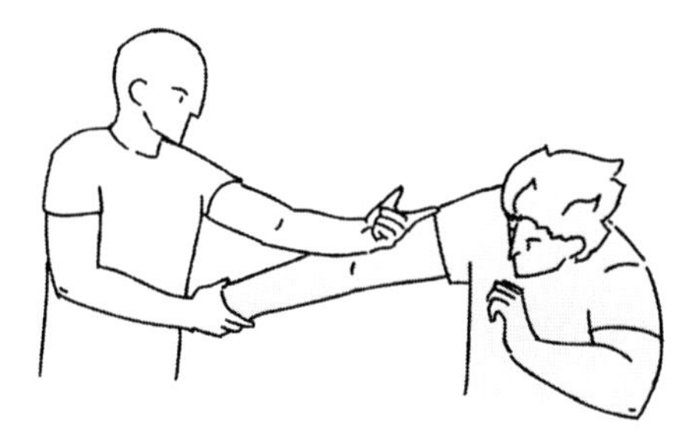

Exercise 26: Lap Sau Arm Lock

Practice using the Lap Sau to apply a basic arm lock.

If your sparring partner grabs you before you apply the pressure, use the Lap Sau change movement to grab his/her arm and pull him/her down to apply pressure to the other arm.

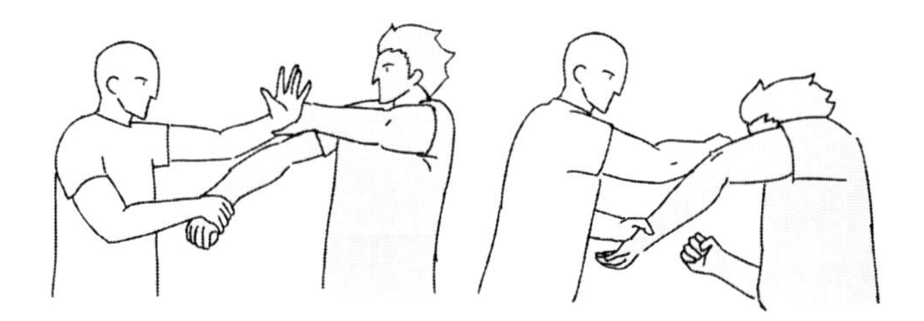

Exercise 27: Lap Sau Arm Lock 2

While attempting the basic arm lock, have your partner grab your wrist then use the Lap Sau change to lock his/her other arm.

Related Chapters:

- Lesson 9: Grabbing
- Lesson 13: Bong Sau

LESSON 15: FOREARM CONDITIONING

This forearm conditioning drill will build your pain tolerance and make your movements faster.

Go lightly to start, so you don't hurt yourself.

Put one hand behind your back and angle the other down to your side. Your partner should do the same. Your hand and arm must be in line, pointed down.

Use your whole body to turn in so that your arms meet in the middle.

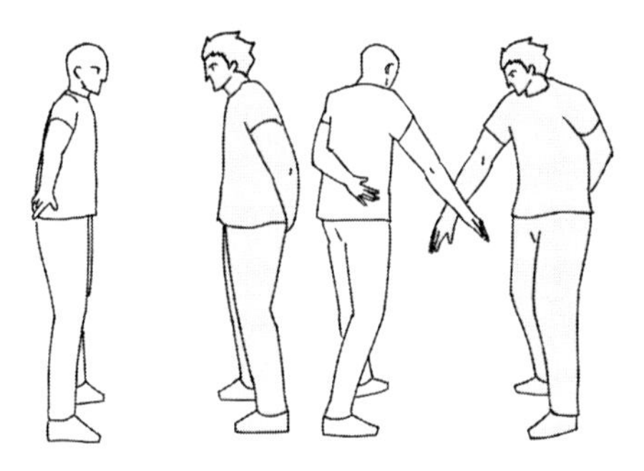

Ensure you use the bony outside part of your forearm. The inner fleshy part will cause you more pain. The following picture shows the wrong way to do it.

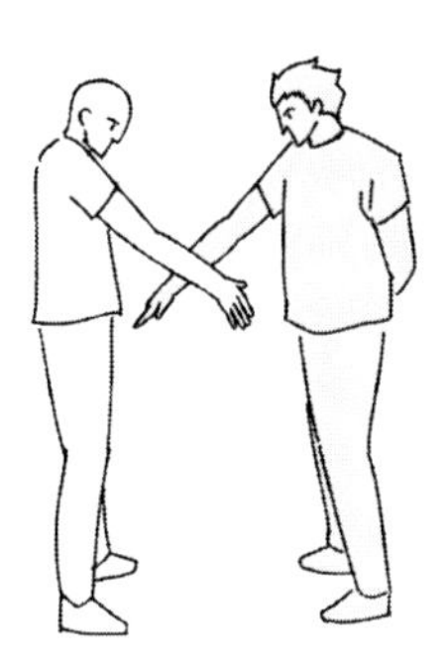

Next, bring your arm in toward your center and up, so your arms meet again.

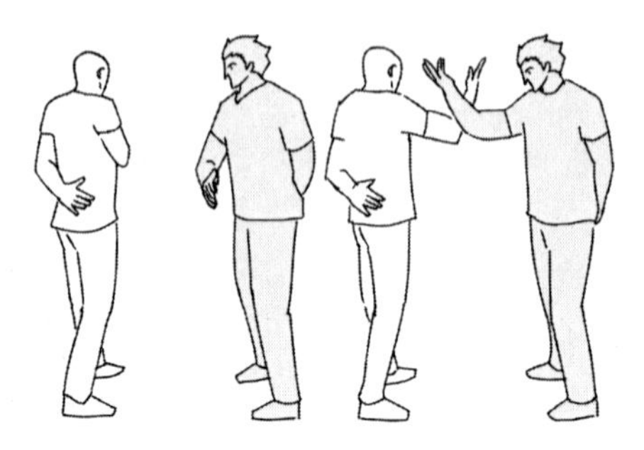

Go back down the same way you came up.

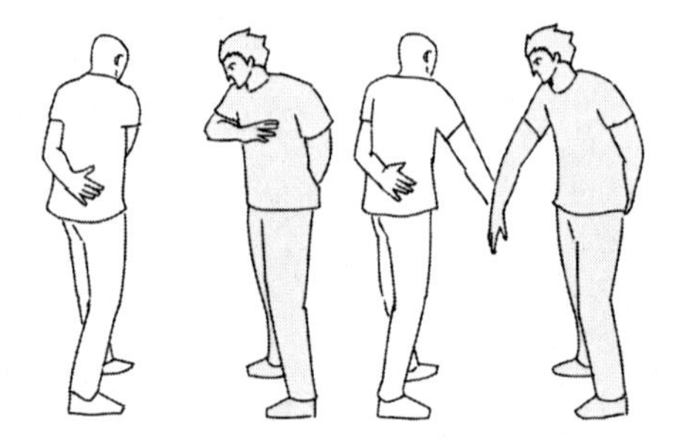

Turn your body to do the same with the other arm.

The pattern is; turn, up, down, turn, up, down.

Exercise 28: Forearm Conditioning

Do the forearm conditioning exercise.

Increase speed and power as you and your partner feel comfortable doing so.

LESSON 16: THE CHOP

This lesson introduces the chop movement for defense and attack. The chop is very useful for causing pain as you defend.

The exercises included in this lesson progressively show how correct body positioning, allowing you to be ready for any attack.

As your opponent attacks with a straight punch, chop down on his/her arm using the same part of your arm that you used in the forearm conditioning exercise. Aim near your opponent's wrist to cause pain.

As soon as you've chopped, use your other hand to grab your opponent's wrist. As you grab him/her, step in and deliver a chop to his/her neck.

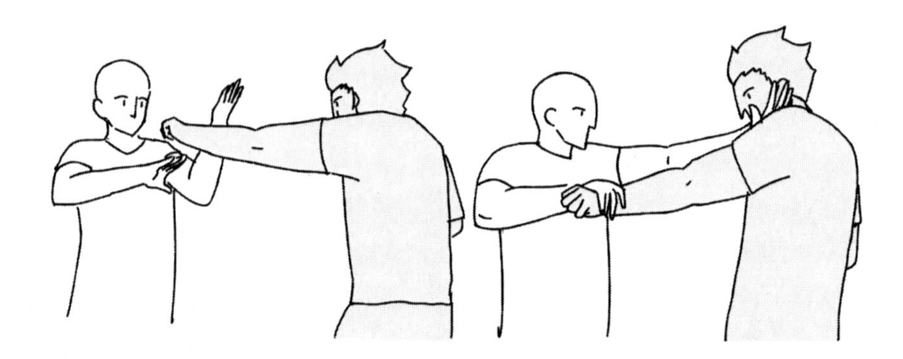

Exercise 29: Chop Defense and Counter

Practice using the chop to defend and counter.

If after the first strike your opponent throws a second punch, take a small step back and use the same arm to defend against it. As you step back, chop his/her neck with your other arm.

Exercise 30: Chop Defense and Counter Extended

Add defense against this follow-up strike to the previous exercise.

If your opponent then uppercuts, bring your elbow down to defend against that.

Ensure you move out of the way, or you'll get hit. If you're too close, you won't have enough room to defend, either.

Exercise 31: Chop Defense and Counter with Uppercut Defense

Add in the uppercut defense to the previous exercise.

If your opponent hooks, just chop again, then attack his/her centerline.

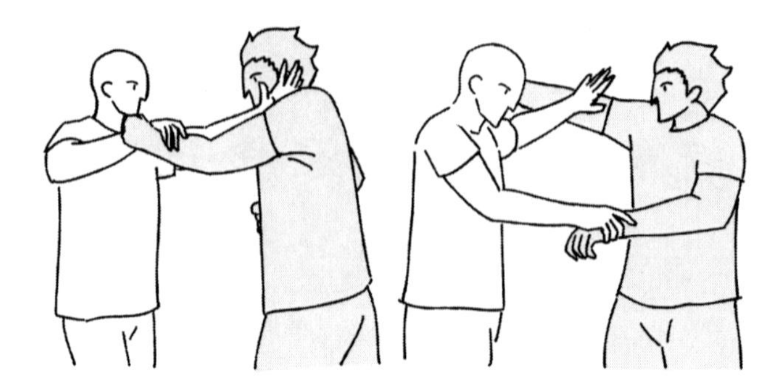

Exercise 32: Chop Defense and Counter with Hook Defense

Replace the uppercut from the previous exercise with a hook, and defend accordingly.

Exercise 33: Chop Defense and Counter with Alternating Uppercut and Hook Defense

Do the chop defense and counter exercise and randomly alternate between the hook and uppercut defenses.

Chopping the Pad

Using a pad means you can focus on applying power to your techniques without hurting your training partner.

As your partner punches, use Tan Sau to defend, then bring your other hand over and pin your opponent's punching hand down. Grab it and force it down. Hold it in tightly; otherwise, he/she will be able to punch you.

Chop the pad.

Don't try to bring your arm back to generate power. That just gives your opponent time to hit you. Instead, use your waist. It's faster and more powerful.

The picture on the right shows the incorrect way to do it.

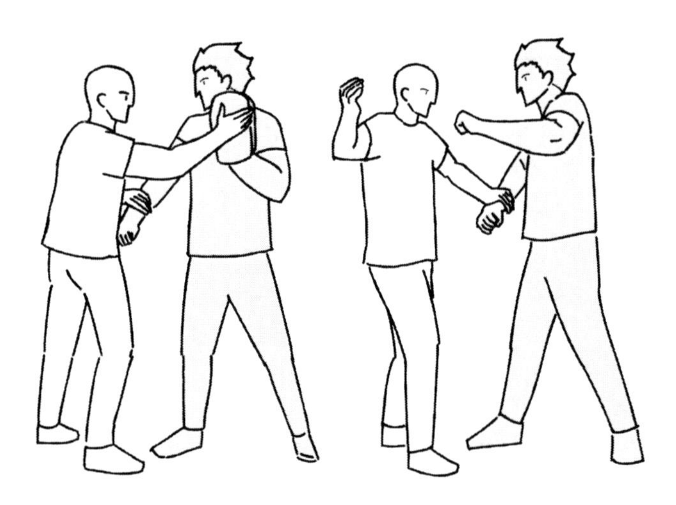

In reality, you would aim for your opponent's neck.

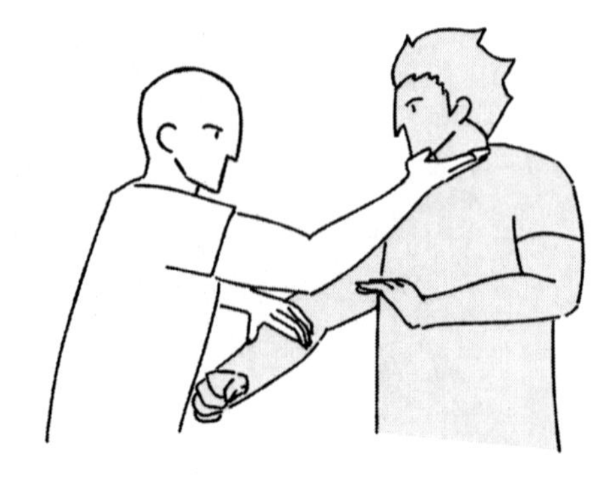

Exercise 34: Chop the Pad

Practice the chop on a pad.

Related Chapters:

- Lesson 7: Tan Sau
- Lesson 15: Forearm Conditioning
- Lesson 17: Uppercut Defense

LESSON 17: UPPERCUT DEFENSE

The previous lesson demonstrated how to defend against the uppercut with your elbow. Here's a way you can defend against the uppercut using the chop.

As your opponent uppercuts, chop down onto his/her arm or wrist. Hitting the wrist will do more damage to him/her, but hitting nearer the elbow will make it easier to counter.

Use your whole body to chop.

Exercise 35: Uppercut Defense

Practice defending against left and right uppercuts using the chop. Use your waist. After the chop, you can counter by attacking straight into your opponent's neck.

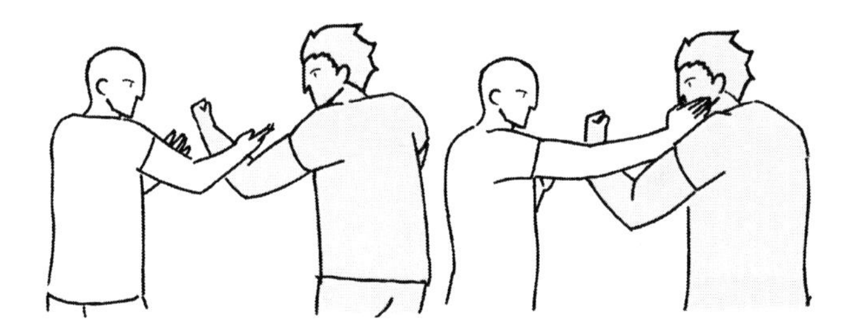

Exercise 36: Uppercut Defense and Counter

Add a counterattack after defending against the uppercut.

Related Chapters:

- Lesson 8: Counterattack
- Lesson 16: The Chop

LESSON 18: TRIPLE DEFENSE

This lesson shows how you can use Tan Sau, Pak Sau, and the chop together to defend against common boxing attacks. The exercise is good for practicing shifting your body weight as your body must turn after each technique.

Your opponent throws a straight punch. Defend with Pak Sau.

He/she throws a cross punch. Defend against it with Pak Sau on the other side.

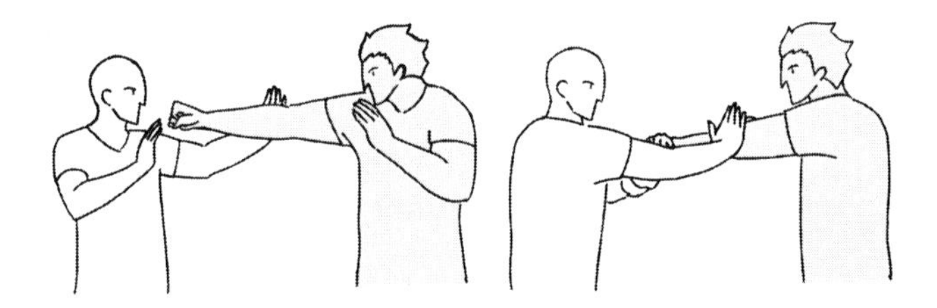

He/she then throws two hooks, one on either side. Use Tan Sau to defend.

Finally your opponent throws two uppercuts. Chop them accordingly.

Exercise 37: Triple Defense

Practice defending against the six attacks in order.

Exercise 38: Triple Defense Random

Have your partner throw straight punches, hooks and uppercuts at random. Defend against them accordingly, with or without counters.

Related Chapters:

- Lesson 7: Tan Sau
- Lesson 10: Pak Sau
- Lesson 16: The Chop

LESSON 19: THREE KICKS

The stomp kick, side kick and front kick are fundamental foot techniques in Wing Chun. This lesson teaches you how to do these three basic kicks on a single spot. It helps you to improve your balance, body position, leg strength, and technique.

Start from the half squat position, and then move into the switching sides position, with approximately 70% of your weight on your rear leg.

Raise your rear leg so your knee is parallel to the floor.

Angle your foot out slightly as you kick your foot out. In a fight, the sole of your foot is what would be hitting the target. The target would be your opponent's thigh or knee. Do not straighten your leg fully; your knee should not lock into place.

This is the stomp kick.

Bring your leg back to the position where your knee is parallel to the floor. Angle your foot slightly in so you can do a side kick that strikes at an imaginary shin target.

Bring your leg back to the position where your knee is parallel to the floor. Thrust it straight out into a front kick. In a fight, your target would be your opponent's gut. Your foot should be vertical.

Bring your leg back and then down to the ground. As you do so, adopt the half squat position.

Turn to your other side and repeat the three kicks with your other leg.

Finally, do the three kicks to the center. Do not turn to the side.

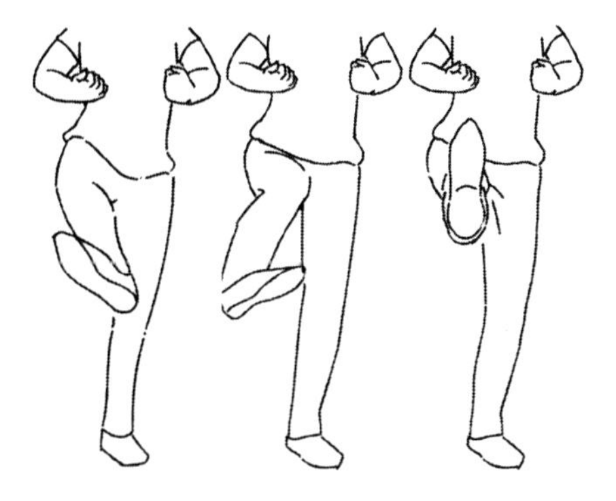

Exercise 39: Three Kicks

Practice the three kicks. As you increase your speed, it will get easier to balance.

Three Kicks Application

This demonstrates the application of the three basic kicks. It also teaches a technique using the same hand to deflect and grab in a fluid motion and emphasizes correct distancing.

As your opponent punches, use a variation of the Tan Sau where your palm is facing away from you. This will enable you to grab your opponent's arm as you defend. As soon as you deflect the punch, grab your opponent's arm and do a stomp kick into his/her shin.

This first kick must be very fast. It will stop the advance and distract him/her.

Bring your leg back and then do a side kick into your opponent's thigh.

Bring your leg back again and then apply the front kick to your opponent's torso, under the armpit. Pull him/her in as you do it and kick upward.

If your distancing is incorrect or you're not stable when performing these kicks, you'll have problems, such as missing your target or becoming unbalanced when he/she pushes into you.

Exercise 40: Three Kicks Application

Practice the three kicks on both sides of the body.

The grabbing technique is hard to apply in a real fight, since it requires very fast reflexes. For now, just do it slowly, to get the movement right. We will revisit it later with speed.

Related Chapters:

- Lesson 1: The Half Squat
- Lesson 7: Tan Sau
- Lesson 9: Grabbing

LESSON 20: STEPPING SIDE KICK

The stepping side kick is useful for attacking an opponent at knee level or below while closing ground. It combines basic stepping with the side kick.

Begin in your fighting stance and step forward a couple of times. When you're ready, plant your rear foot firmly into the ground as it comes up so you can do the side kick with your lead leg. Drop your foot back to the ground and then repeat the process.

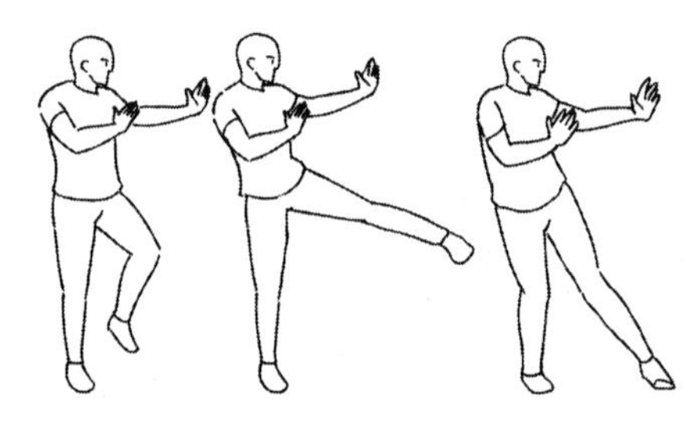

Do this a few times and then use switching sides to turn around so you can do it using your other side. Here is the view from the front, so you can see the alignment of the body with the hands.

Exercise 41: Stepping Side Kick

Practice the stepping side kick on both sides of your body. Step forward two or three times and then kick.

LESSON 21: PUNCH ROLL

The punch roll is a basic Wing Chun drill which is beneficial for many things, such as increasing speed, honing reflexes, understanding the line of the body, trapping, and closing distance.

The punch roll can be broken down into four movements: defend, under, cover, and punch.

Your partner punches at you and you defend with Pak Sau.

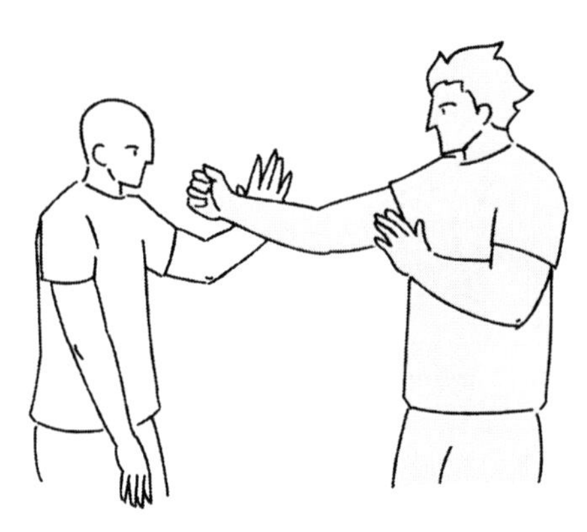

You then move your other hand under his/her arm to deflect it out of the way.

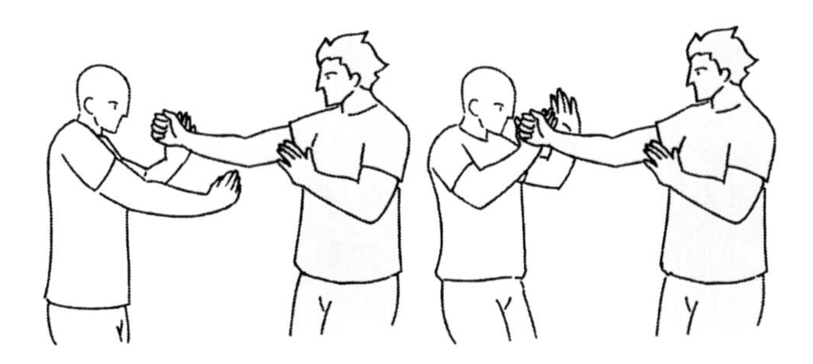

You then bring the hand that you did the Pak Sau with over to cover his/her arm and force it down.

Finally, you punch and your partner uses Pak Sau to defend.

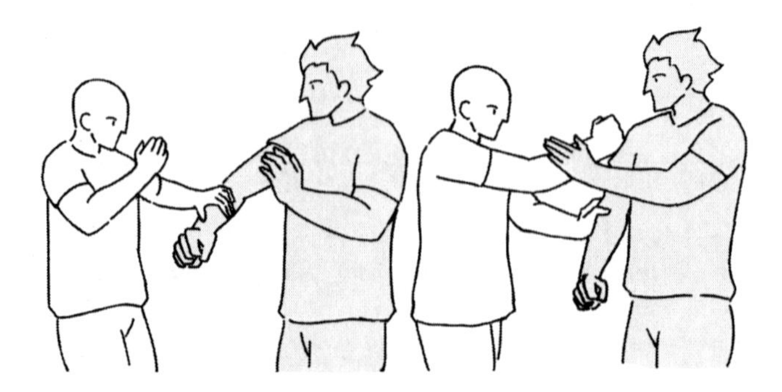

You repeat this defend, under, cover, and punch routine between you and you partner.

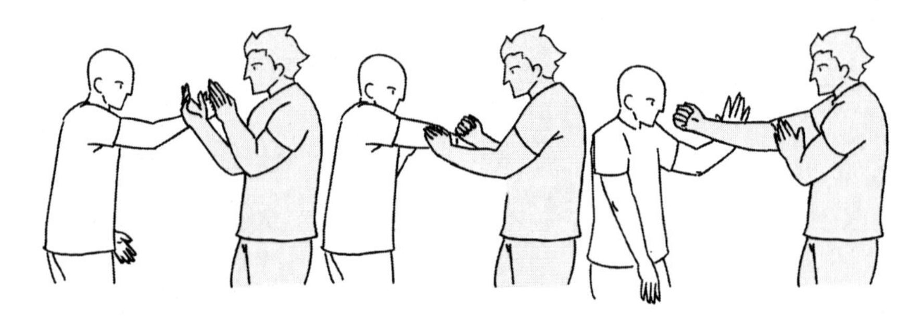

Although it's presented here in four separate movements, the punch roll is fluid. There should be no discernable pause between the movements. They should roll into each other.

The punch roll can also be done without Pak Sau. Instead, you'll use the "under" as the initial defending maneuver.

When you first begin to practice the punch roll, you have to make sure you're ready. Every time your partner punches, you must be ready to react. After some practice, it will become instinctive.

Exercise 42: Punch Roll

Practice the punch roll on both sides.

Punch Roll Change

Once you're confident with doing the punch roll on both sides of your body, you can advance to changing sides while doing the punch roll, as opposed to stopping, changing sides, and then restarting. It allows you to change from left to right (or vice versa) very quickly.

The movement needed to change can be broken down into four stages: chop, under, cover, punch. As with the punch roll, these four movements should be done with no pause between them.

Begin by doing the punch roll as normal. When you're ready to change, instead of punching, chop the hand that your partner would usually use to intercept your punch.

Next, bring your other hand under and to the outside of his/hers.

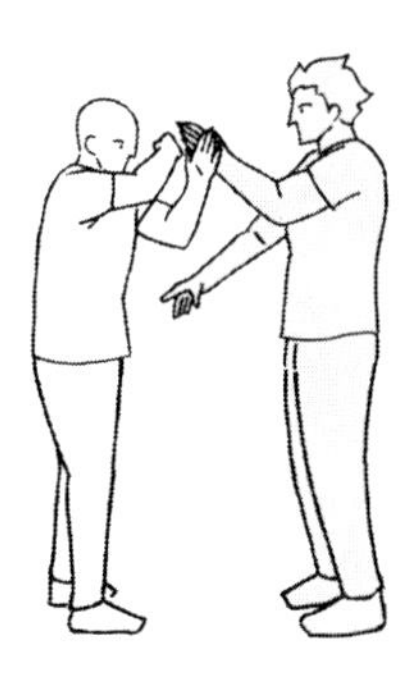

Cover his/her hand with the one you used to chop, and then punch.

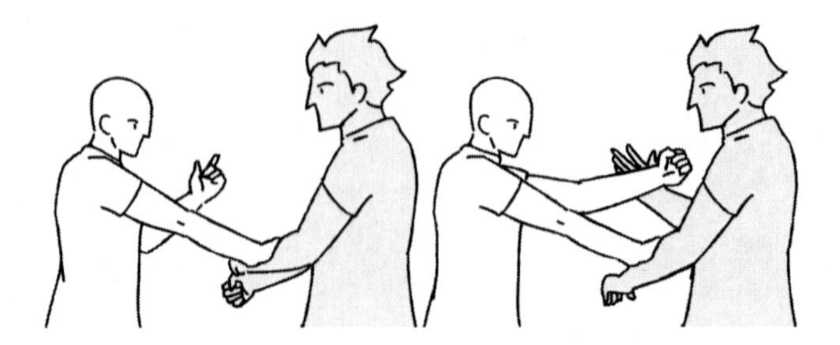

From here, continue the punch roll on the new side.

In a real right, your chop would be to your opponent's neck.

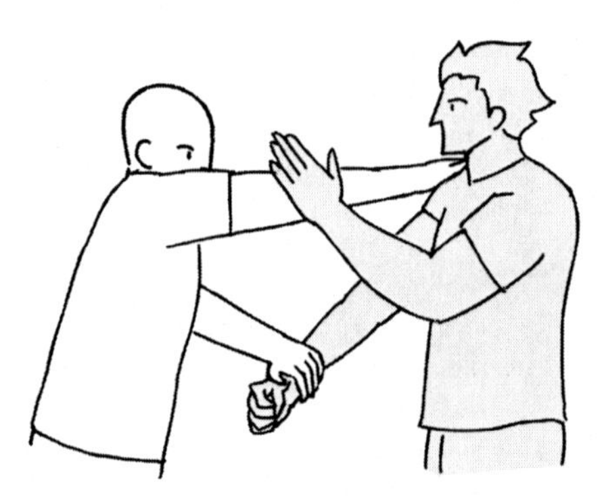

Exercise 43: Punch Roll Change

Practice the punch roll with this change.

Practice the punch roll often. You want it to be instinctive, so you no longer need to think about what your hands are doing. Your mind will then be free to think ahead.

Related Chapters:

- Lesson 10: Pak Sau

LESSON 22: TRAPPING

Trapping is an important concept in Wing Chun. It is when you immobilize your opponent to keep him/her from attacking and defending while still being able to attack him/her yourself. Many defensive techniques, grabs, holds, pressing etc., can be considered as trapping.

> "Greet what arrives, escort what leaves and rush upon loss of contact."
>
> Yip Man.

It's important to note that in a real fight or fast-paced sparring, it's the simple traps, such as defending, grabbing, and punching, that work best.

Here's a basic method of trapping both of your opponent's hands. It's very closely related to the punch roll, and helps you learn to feel your opponent's movements.

Your opponent strikes and you deflect with Tan Sau. At the same time, you bring your other hand over to pin his/her arm down.

As you pin the arm down, you punch. As you punch, your opponent defends.

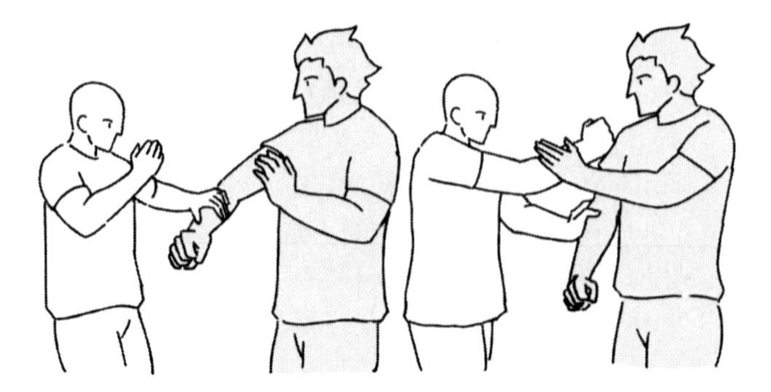

As soon as your opponent's hand touches yours, bring your non-punching hand over to pin this hand down on top of his/her other one. Strike.

In training, hit your opponent's body. In a real fight, hit his/her throat.

Maintain the correct distance.

When you punch, remember to keep upright and generate power from your waist. If your opponent moves back, follow him/her in by stepping forward as opposed to leaning in, which will cause you to lose balance and power.

Your first punch is bait for your opponent to defend against so you can trap the second hand. The reason you don't just hit your opponent the first time is because you could also be hit. You will just be trading punches.

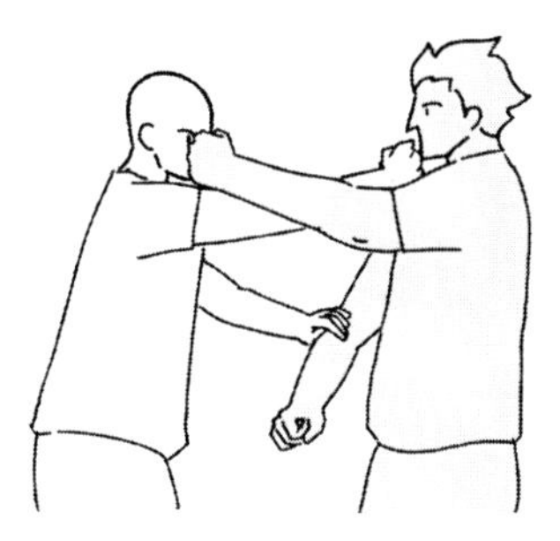

Exercise 44: Trapping

Practice this method of trapping both of your opponent's arms.

Trapping Complications

Hold his/her arms down tightly and put some force into the hold; otherwise, he/she will just lift them up.

If your opponent does manage to push your arms up, you can punch his/her stomach.

If he/she hooks, you can defend and punch.

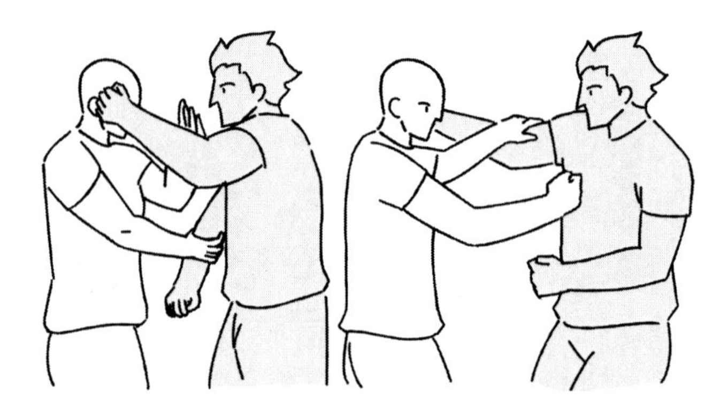

Exercise 45: Trapping Complications

Practice trapping and have your partner throw another one or two random attacks for you to defend against.

Trapping Multi-Punch

Once you're comfortable with this lesson's initial method of trapping, you can add in more attacks such as repeating punches.

Trap and punch as previously explained.

You then bring your punching hand down to hold his/her arms down while you punch with your other hand. You can continue punching with alternating hands in this manner.

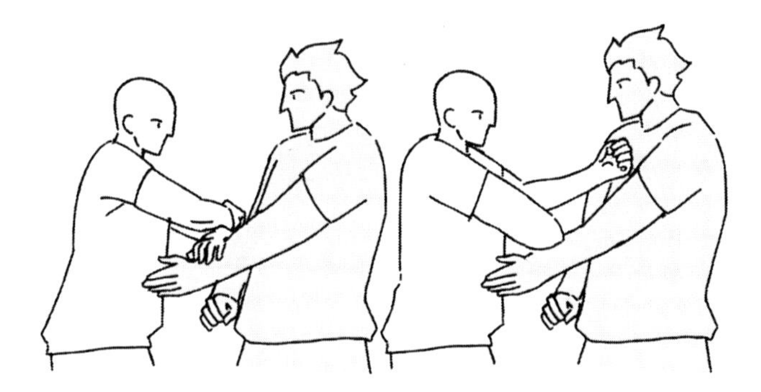

After every punch, your opponent will move back a little. Use footwork to maintain your distance. Do not lean in.

Exercise 46: Trapping Multi-Punch

Trap both your partner's arms and then do three punches.

Trapping Elbow

This replaces the punch with an elbow.

Trap your opponent's hands as in the previous exercises. Drive your elbow into his/her chest. Keep your elbow in line and move forward with your body upright. Create power with footwork. Push your body into the strike

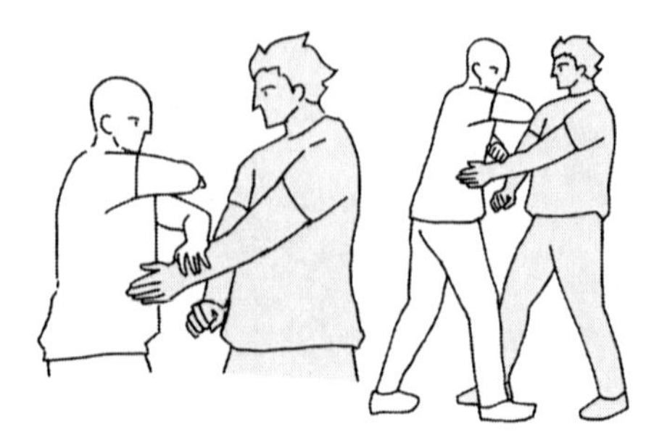

Don't lean in or try to go too high. You'll lose balance and power.

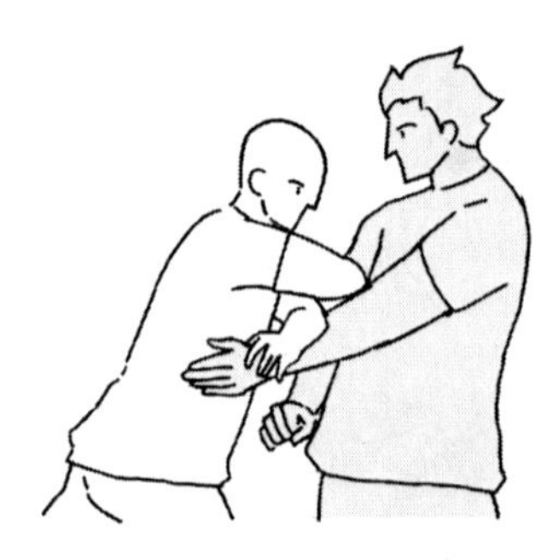

Exercise 47: Trapping Elbow

Practice trapping and then attacking with the elbow. Do not go too hard on your training partner. Even if your partner is wearing a body pad (which he/she should be), a strong elbow will do damage.

Trapping with Pads

When practicing trapping and attacking with pads, you can apply more power than if you were just using a body pad, but you can only trap one hand.

If you're using an elbow, make sure your partner holds the pad square on, or you'll miss and hit him/her in the chest. Practice slowly at first.

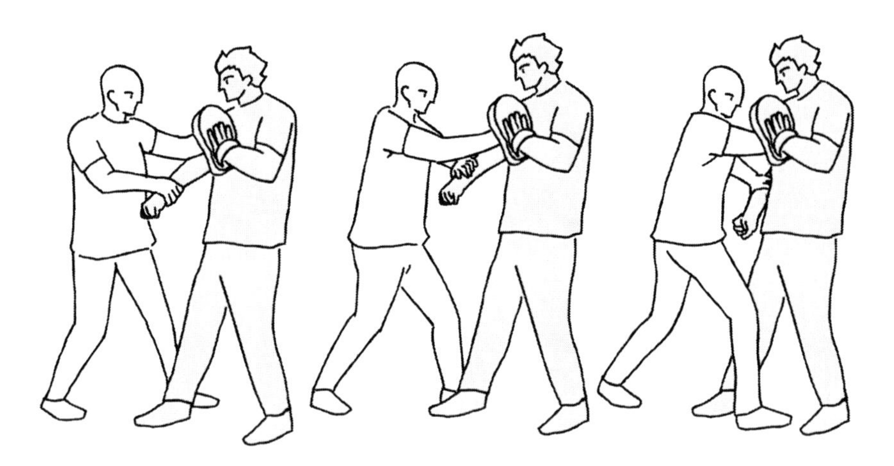

Exercise 48: Trapping with Pads

Practice trapping and hitting using hand pads.

Related Chapters:

- Lesson 7: Tan Sau
- Lesson 9: Grabbing
- Lesson 21: Punch Roll

LESSON 23: WRIST GRAB ESCAPE

This exercise demonstrates a basic wrist-grab escape. It uses the previous trapping exercise as a scenario, but is also the basis for ways of escaping someone's grip in most cases.

Begin with the trapping exercise, as previously described. When you try to do the second punch, you'll find that your opponent has grabbed your wrist so tightly that you can't easily pin them down.

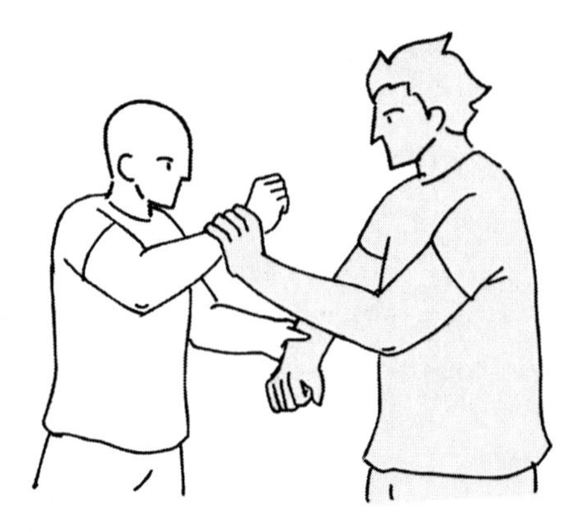

React quickly. Lift your elbow parallel to the ground and then drive it forward into him/her.

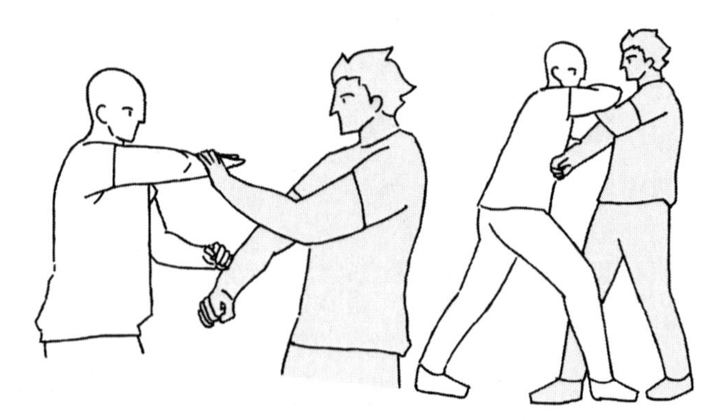

If your opponent's grip is so strong that you can't raise your elbow, just bring your hand up a little and hit the inside of his/her forearm to break the grip and attack. It works because you are forcing your arm out at the weakest point of your opponent's grip, where the thumb and fingers (would) meet.

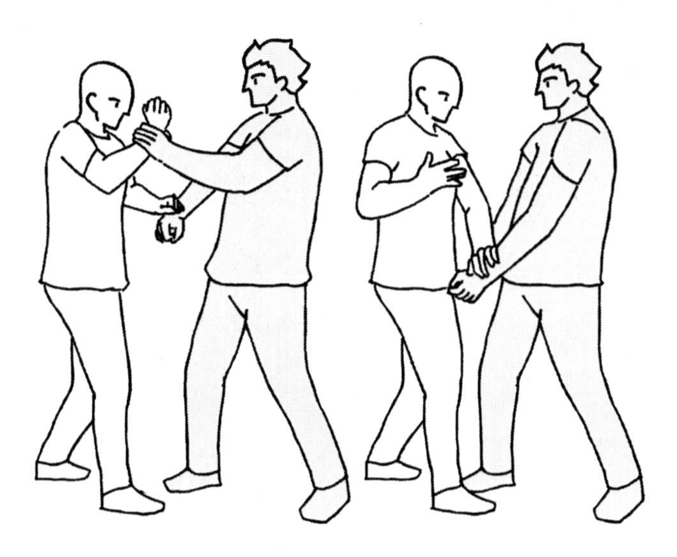

Exercise 49: Wrist Grab Escape

Practice the various wrist grab escapes.

Related Chapters:

- Lesson 22: Trapping

LESSON 24: PUNCH ROLL LAP SAU INTERCHANGE

This lesson demonstrates how you can flow between the punch roll and Lap Sau drills.

Punch Roll to Lap Sau

Begin with the punch roll.

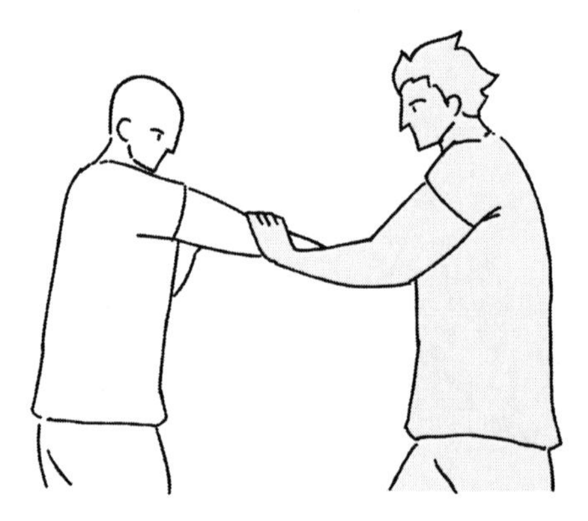

When you are ready, grab your partner's punch and move into Lap Sau.

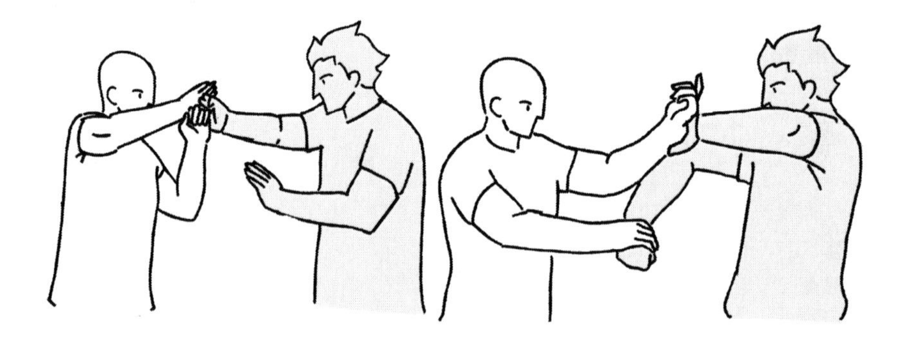

Lap Sau to Punch Roll

As you bring your partner's hand down, bring your other hand over to pin it down.

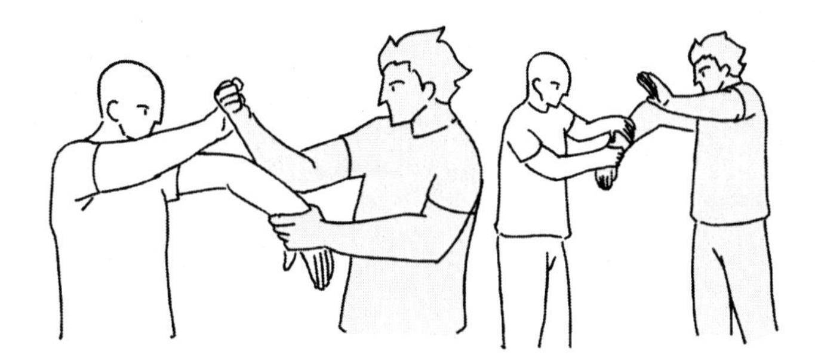

As you pin it, punch.

Exercise 50: Punch Roll Lap Sau Interchange

Practice changing between the punch roll and Lap Sau. When comfortable, start changing sides during each of the separate drills.

Related Chapters:

- Lesson 14: Lap Sau Drill
- Lesson 21: Punch Roll

LESSON 25: KAU SAU

Kau Sau (detaining hand) is a Wing Chun hand position. It's a combination of Fut Sau (low) and either Tan Sau or Pak Sau (high). Here it is demonstrated with Pak Sau.

Fut Sau (outward palm arm) rises outward and upward from the center of the body. In this demonstration, it's performed to the side, to defend against an attack. Pak Sau and Fut Sau occur together with the Pak Sau rising out and the Fut Sau sweeping from the center.

Using the Kau Sau, as demonstrated here, requires whole-body movement.

Begin in the half squat position, with your hands up. Move your lower hand down and rotate the upper hand inward.

Use changing sides to rotate your body to whichever side your bottom hand is on. Ensure your top hand is in line, and don't put it too close to your face. It needs space to stop the strike.

The idea is that your top hand will protect the upper portion of your torso and your bottom hand will protect the lower.

Next, angle your top hand down and angle your bottom hand up.

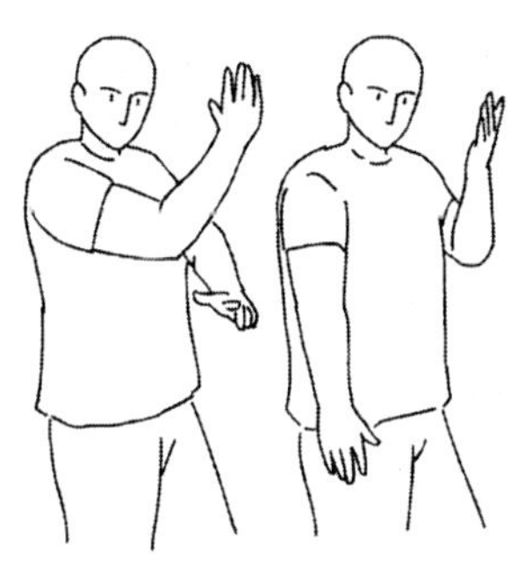

Rotate your body to the other side. Your whole body must be strong to prevent attacks getting through. You must be stable and your arms strong in place.

Your change of hands and the movement of your body should happen as one movement. Remember, it's the motion of your whole body that creates the force behind your movements, not just the motion of your arm.

Exercise 51: Kau Sau

Practice this version of the Kau Sau from left to right and vice versa.

Related Chapters:

- Lesson 1: The Half Squat
- Lesson 7: Tan Sau
- Lesson 10: Pak Sau

LESSON 26: SIDE KICK DEFENSE

This shows how the lower arm of the Kau Sau can be used to defend against a side kick to the stomach.

As your opponent side kicks to your stomach, step back and use Fut Sau to chop his/her lower leg.

Make sure you turn your body to the side, or you'll get hit. Stepping back will help you to absorb the impact.

The chop can be done either side of the leg, but hitting the back of his/her calf will cause your opponent the most pain.

Exercise 52: Side Kick Defense

Practice defending against side kicks with Fut Sau. Step back on each kick, so you practice on both sides.

Once you've intercepted the kick, you may end up on the outside of your opponent's guard. This is a good time to attack.

LESSON 27: ROUND KICK DEFENSE

This demonstrates using the Pak Sau motion from Kau Sau to defend against a round kick.

As your opponent kicks, press your elbow/upper forearm into his/her lower leg. Ensure your feet are grounded for stability and that you turn your body to avoid the blow.

Your elbow can land anywhere on your opponent's lower leg, but hitting him/her on the ankle will inflict the most damage.

Exercise 53: Round Kick Defense

Practice defending against the round kick with this modified Pak Sau.

Step back on each kick so that you practice on both sides.

Related Chapters:

- Lesson 10: Pak Sau
- Lesson 25: Kau Sau

LESSON 28: GUM SAU

Gum Sau (pressing hand) is a great defensive technique to use against rising attacks such as uppercuts and kicks.

This lesson demonstrates using Gum Sau to defend against a front kick.

As the front kick comes in, step back and turn as you strike down at an angle, driving the side of your palm into his/her ankle. In training, aim for his/her shin.

You have to be strong in your movement. If you just slap at it, as in the picture on the right, you'll get hurt.

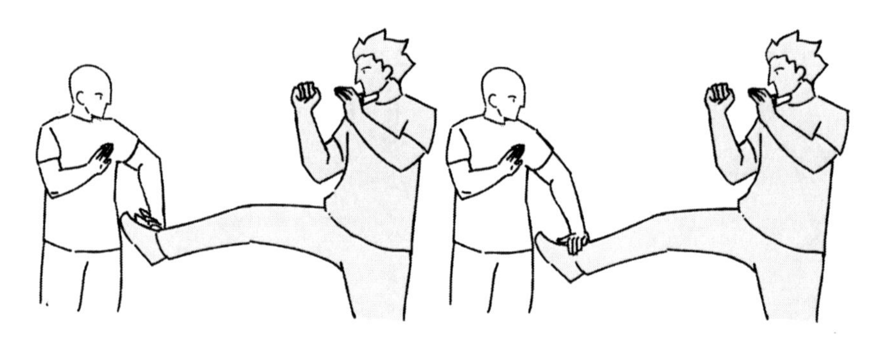

Be sure to turn so you're out of the way and in line to counter.

Exercise 54: Front Kick Defense

Practice using the Gum Sau to defend against front kicks. Step back on each kick so you practice on both sides.

Exercise 55: Random Kick Defense

Practice defending against side, round, and front kicks at random.

LESSON 29: ELBOW DRILL

This is another Wing Chun drill to help increase response time, muscle memory, etc.

Your partner comes in to elbow you. Step back and use your hand to defend. Stepping back helps to absorb the strike. If you don't step back, you'll probably get hurt.

You then bring your other hand up from underneath.

Use your first hand to pin your opponent's elbow down.

Now step forward to elbow him/her. Don't lean in. Keep yourself upright and use your whole body to produce power.

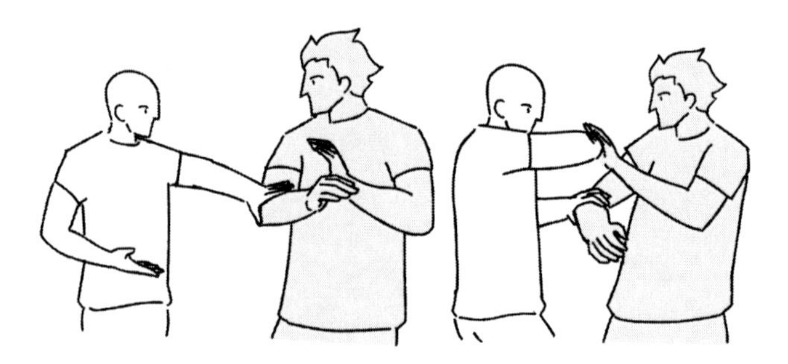

As you come in, your partner steps back and defends. This back and forth continues.

Exercise 56: Elbow Drill

Practice the elbow drill on both sides.

Elbow Drill Change

This shows how you can change sides while doing the elbow drill. It uses a similar method as when changing sides during the punch roll.

When you pin your opponent's arm down, instead of returning an elbow, use a chop.

Then bring your other hand from underneath to change sides. Be sure to change your lead leg at the same time.

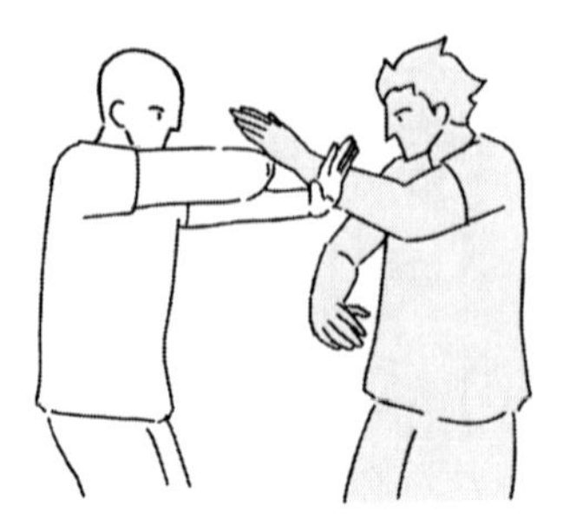

Pin your opponent's arm down and elbow.

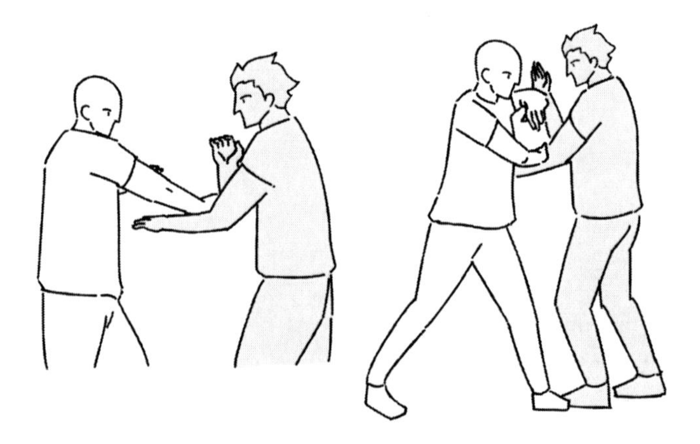

Exercise 57: Elbow Drill Change

Do the elbow drill, incorporating the movements to swap sides.

Related Chapters:

- Lesson 21: Punch Roll

LESSON 30: INTERCEPTING KICKS

Interception is an important concept in Wing Chun. It is where you use an attack to defend. In fact, where most other martial art styles use blocks, Wing Chun uses interceptions.

This lesson shows how you can intercept various attacks/advances with various kicks.

The kick you use will depend on your distance and the attack made on you.

Intercepting Stomp Kick

The stomp kick can be used to effectively stop a low Thai-style round kick. As the kick comes in, use the sole of your foot to intercept it at the shin.

Keep your body upright and lean in a little as you do the kick. If you lean back, your opponent will be able to push you over, as in the picture on the left. Leaning in also makes it easier to follow up.

If you're too close, it won't work, because you won't have enough room to do the movement.

Exercise 58: Intercepting Stomp Kick

Practice intercepting the round kick with your stomp kick. Ensure you give yourself enough distance to time the interception correctly.

Intercepting Side Kick

The side kick is useful for intercepting an opponent's advance.

When your opponent wants to hit you, he/she has to come towards you, and in order to do so, he/she has to move his/her leg first.

Side kick his/her shin or knee as he/she moves in. It's a flicking kick to stop the advance, not a finishing move.

When you intercept his/her leg, the accompanying punch will most likely be out of range to hit you, but you can defend against your opponent's arm at the same time if you want.

Exercise 59: Intercepting Side Kick

Practice using the side kick to intercept an advance.

LESSON 31: LOW KICK, HIGH KICK DEFENSE

This exercise uses the intercepting stomp and the modified Pak Sau from lesson 27 (round kick defense) to defend against the low kick, high kick combination which is common amongst Muay-Thai-style fighters.

It's a good illustration of the economy of motion concept:

- When attacked below the waist, you defend with your legs and feet.
- When attacked above the waist. you defend with your hands.

When you're close to your opponent, he/she has no room to kick you high. If he/she wants to kick, he/she has to go low. Intercept with a stomp kick and then step back.

Stepping back creates the distance your opponent needs to kick you high.

When he/she follows up with the second kick, use the modified Pak Sau from lesson 27 (round kick defense) to defend.

Exercise 60: Low Kick, High Kick Defense

Practice this low kick, high kick defense on both sides of your body.

Related Chapters:

- Lesson 27: Round Kick Defense

LESSON 32: PUNCH ROLL/ELBOW DRILL INTERCHANGE

This demonstrates how to link the punch roll with the elbow drill.

Punch Roll to Elbow Drill

Start with the punch roll. Chop to change sides and come underneath with your other hand.

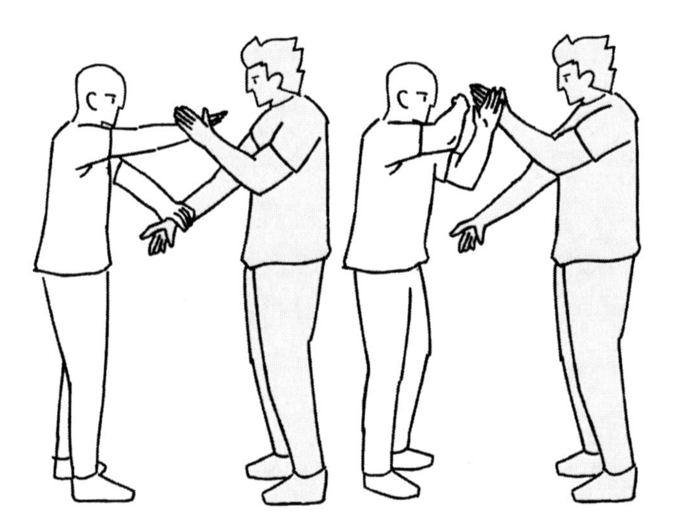

Pin your opponent's arm down and then elbow him/her.

Elbow Drill to Punch Roll

As you chop to change, bring your other hand under.

Pin his/her arm down and punch.

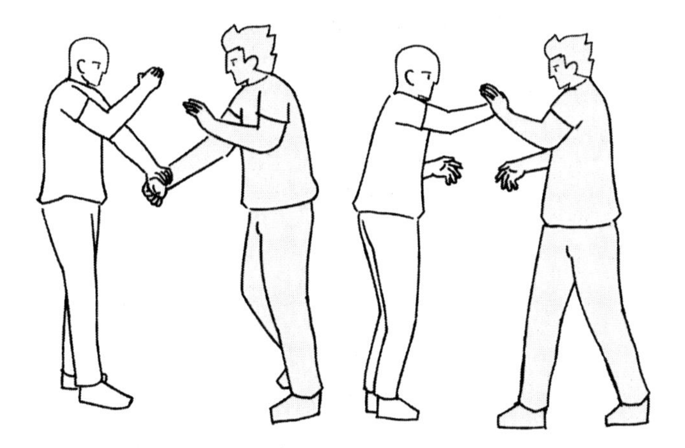

Exercise 61: Punch Roll Elbow Drill Interchange

Practice changing between the punch roll and the elbow drill.

When you're comfortable with the interchange, add changing sides during each of the separate drills.

Exercise 62: Three Drills

Move between the Lap Sau, punch roll and elbow drills.

Begin with the punch roll. Change sides a few times and then change to Lap Sau.

Change sides a few times during Lap Sau and then change back to the punch roll.

When you're ready, change to the elbow drill and then back to the punch roll.

Change sides during any of the drills when you feel like it.

Once you're proficient at these three drills, you won't have to think about them. You'll just feel the movement and react accordingly.

Bonus: Basic Chi Sao

Another drill that can be linked is Chi Sao (sticky hands).

Chi Sao is an advanced Wing Chun drill used to improve touch sensitivity and harnesses flowing energy (chi). It also increases body balance and promotes the looseness of the arms and body.

Chi Sao is not covered in detail in this book and is not included in the training schedule. A few chapters from *How to Do Chi Sao* by Sam Fury are included now as a bonus. These chapters are enough for you to learn how to be able to do the basic Chi Sao drill.

www.SurvivalFitnessPlan.com/Chi-Sao

Hand Positions

There are three main hand positions used in Chi Sao. They are Tan Sao (Palm up Block/Taun Sao), Bong Sau (Wing Arm Block/Bon Sao) and Fook Sao (Bridge-On Arm Block/Fok Sao/Fuk Sao).

Practice each of these hand positions separately as well as switching from one to the other.

Tan Sao

Tan Sao is used to limit the opponent's ability to strike straight in. Drive it forward from the center of your body in a slight upward motion.

Ensure that:

- Your palm is open, fairly flat and facing the sky.
- There is approximately a 30-degree bend in your elbow.
- Your whole arm is very slightly angled towards your centerline.

Bong Sau

Bong Sau is used to redirect the opponent's attack to a neutral position. It's best used when you're already in contact with the opponent's arm.

Ensure that:

- Your elbow is pointed straight out and angled slightly towards your body.
- Your forearm is angled at a 45-degree downward slope in towards the centerline.
- Your forearm is also angled 45 degrees forward.
- Your wrist is on your centerline.
- Your elbow is higher than your wrist.
- Your hand/fingers point in the same direction as your forearm.
- Your upper arm is in a fairly straight line, pointing to the front.
- The angle of your elbow is slightly greater than 90 degrees.

Fook Sao

In this defensive position, your arm is placed over your opponent's arm. The exact positioning is adjusted to fit the situation and is often described as either high or low.

Ensure that:

- Your elbow is about 6-8 inches from your body and angles in towards the center of it.
- Your forearm is angled up, with the hand open and the fingers hooked down towards your wrist.

Dan Chi Sao

The movements in this drill are not to be applied with intent of striking. They are for teaching the feeling of movement and, to begin with, are to be performed gently.

Contrary to the name, it is the forearms that "stick," not the hands. They stay touching throughout the entire drill.

P1's right arm is in Tan Sao. P2 adopts Fook Sao, with his left arm on top of P1's arm. He then presses his elbow inwards, towards his centerline. Both exert a slight forward pressure.

In one motion, P1 uses Tan Sao to guide P2's left arm off the centerline, then attempts to strike with the same hand.

P2 defends by dropping his elbow down and inward.

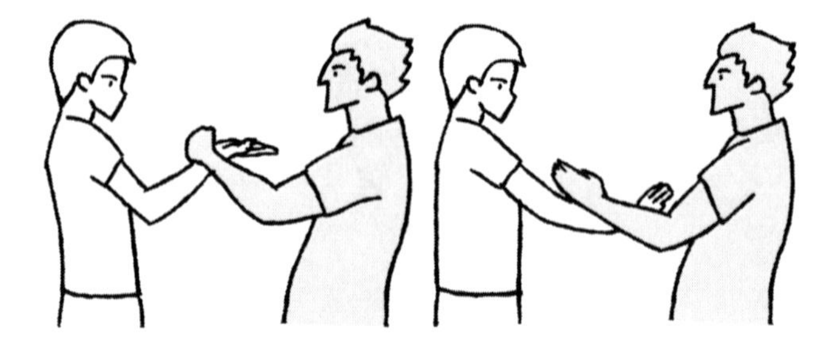

P2 attempts to strike P1's face. P1 defends with Bong Sao. P1 and P2 return to the starting position. They repeat the drill.

Double Dan Chi Sao

This is the same as Dan Chi Sao, but with P1's free hand in a Low Fook Sao over P2's Tan Sao. This position does not change, while P1 performs Dan Chi Sao as normal with the other hand.

At the end of one complete round, switch arms. Practice until the switch between arms is seamless.

Luk Sao

Luk Sao is the base of Chi Sao. Practice it on its own until it's fluid before incorporating attack and defense drills. Throughout the movement, keep your shoulders relaxed and apply a slight forward pressure.

Note: If your hand positions are correct, forward pressure will be maintained automatically. If your opponent removes opposing pressure, your hand will strike forward by reflex.

Luk Sao is basically a move between two positions: from Bong Sao and Low Fook Sao to High Fook Sao and Tan Sao.

P1's right hand is in Tan Sao. P2's right hand is in Bong Sao. Both of their left arms are in the Fook Sao position, situated over their partners' opposite arms (right on left, left on right).

P1's Fook Sao is in a high position, while P2's is low. The elbows of arms with which they're performing Fook Sao should be constantly pressed into the centerline.

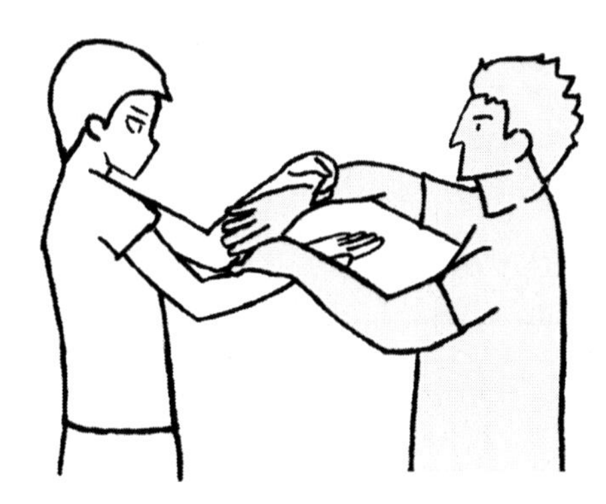

P1 rotates his right elbow up, keeping the wrist in towards his centerline. As his elbow rises up to shoulder height, his forearm drops into Bong Sao. His left hand stays in Fook Sao throughout the movement, but moves to a low position. Keep the elbow down on the Fook Sao or forward pressure will be lost.

As P1 does the above, P2 drops his Bong Sao back down into Tan Sao. As his Bong Sao drops, he moves his wrist outward and the elbow lowers back into its drawn-in position of Tan Sao. As his Bong Sao settles into a Tan Sao, his Fook Sao moves from low to high while staying in contact with P1's right Bong Sao.

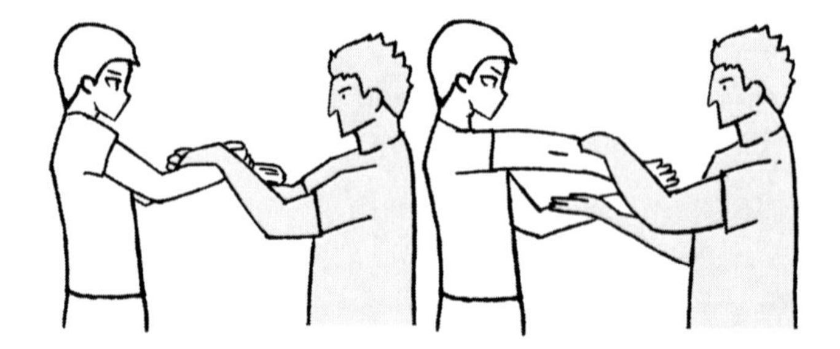

They then reverse the roll and return to the starting position.

All this is done in a flowing manner, and it is important to do it with intent. Turn and push to interlock the hands. Be tense but flexible.

All drills outlined from now on start from Luk Sao, unless otherwise stated. When explanations of when to initiate a drill sequence from Luk Sao are given, the terms "high or low point/position" are used. This does not mean the movement is to be started at the very highest or lowest point.

The exact point where one should begin a technique is impossible to describe. With practice, you'll discover the best timing.

Lap Sau to Chi Sao Interchange

During Lap Sau, as you bring your opponent's arm down, follow it with your other arm.

Bring your other arm in and begin Chi Sao.

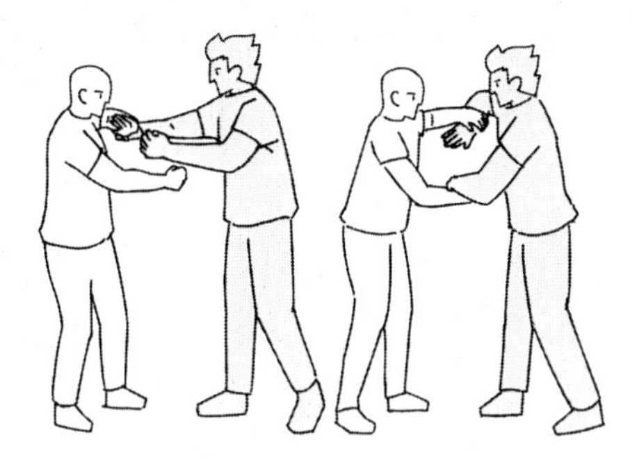

Chi Sao to Punch Roll

During Chi Sao, bring your hand under your opponent's arm, then pin it down and go into the punch roll.

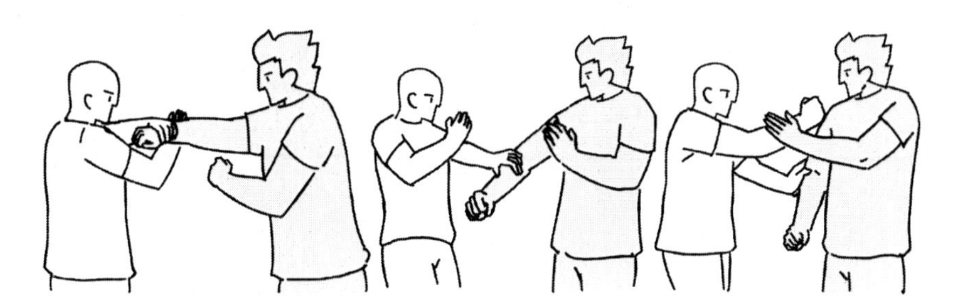

Related Chapters:

- Lesson 13: Bong Sau
- Lesson 21: Punch Roll
- Lesson 29: Elbow Drill

LESSON 33: BIU SAU

Biu Sau (darting hand) is a useful Wing Chun technique for deflection, attacking, or simultaneous attack and defense.

Traditionally, Biu Sau comes directly from your centerline. It is a perfect example of the direct-line concept.

In this lesson, Biu Sau's use is demonstrated against the common jab-cross combination.

For this to be effective, you must be fast and maintain a good distance.

As the jab comes in, you move to the outside and deflect it with a modified Biu Sau, coming over it with your hand.

When the cross comes in, you have to change sides. Use the same hand to come underneath the cross and go directly for your opponent's eyes. It will place you on the outside of his/her guard, which is a perfect position for you to attack from.

If you can't go straight for your opponent's eyes, attack his/her ribs instead.

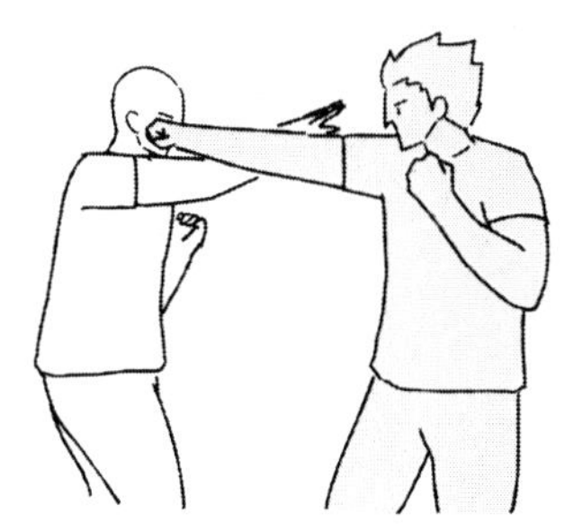

Here, you can see the proper position for your feet. Move as needed to avoid being hit.

Exercise 63: Jab-Cross Defense

Practice using this modified Biu Sau to defend against the jab-cross combination.

LESSON 34: BOXING DEFENSE

On the street, most people fight in a manner similar to boxing. It makes sense to learn how to defend against the common boxing attacks.

As your opponent throws a straight punch, move out of the way and palm it down. As the second straight punch comes in, move back and palm it down as well.

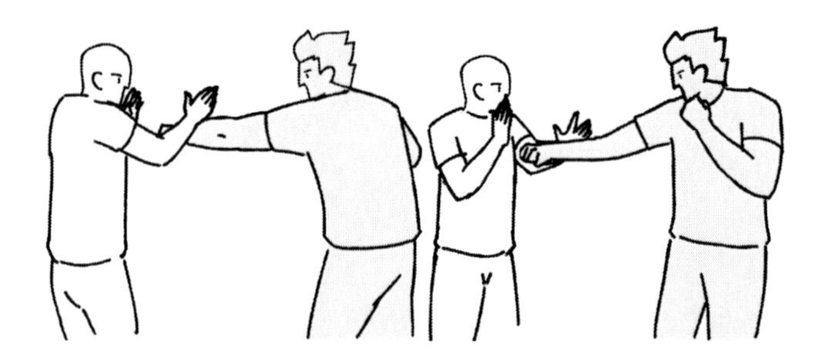

Next, your opponent throws body punches. Defend by dropping your elbows to cover your ribs, and move back as the punches come in. You will probably need to do this for every punch.

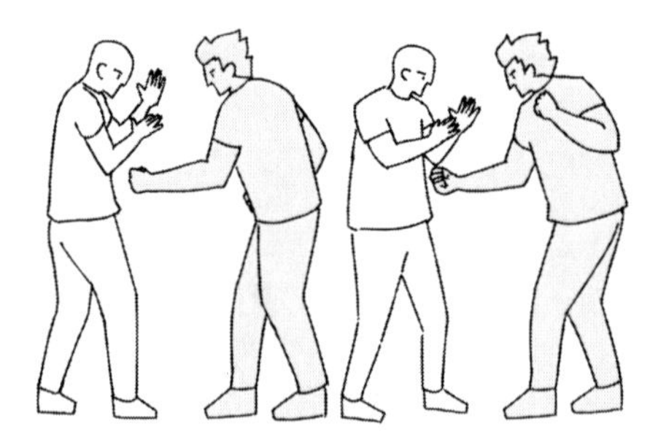

Next are hooks to the head. Move your arm up so your forearm meets your opponent's wrist.

Finally, there are the uppercuts. Use your palm to stop them.

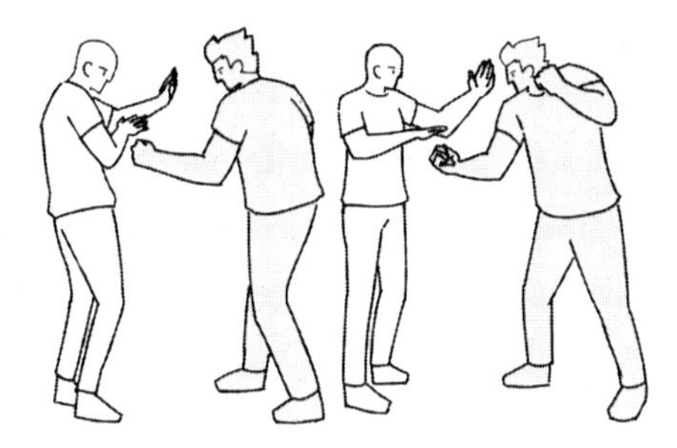

Exercise 64: Boxing Defense

Practice defending against the basic boxing punches.

Exercise 65: Random Boxing Defense

Have your partner mix up the order of the punches. Move freely and counter when you see an opportunity.

LESSON 35: PUNCH ROLL KICKS

Hopefully you have been practicing the punch roll regularly and the motion is now somewhat instinctive. Now you can add in kicks.

Punch Roll with Drop Kick

The drop kick is best to use when you're too close for the side kick and you're attacking someone below the waist.

Start with the punch roll and go to change sides.

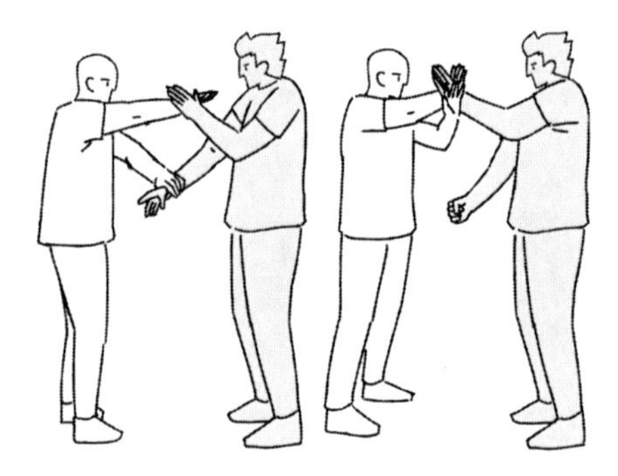

When you grab your opponent, put in a drop kick to his/her thigh or knee. The rhythm is chop, grab, and kick.

Don't lean back. If you aren't grounded with your body upright, your opponent can push you over. If anything, lean in a little.

Exercise 66: Punch Roll with Drop Kick

Practice the punch roll with the drop kick. When you're comfortable, move around as you do it.

Punch Roll with Side Kick

This is how to incorporate the side kick with the punch roll. If you're close, the side kick won't work. You'll be unbalanced. If this is the case, use the drop kick instead.

As you change your hands over during the punch roll, grab your opponent. Turn and side kick him/her.

Don't lean back. Keep your body upright.

Exercise 67: Punch Roll with Side Kick

Practice the punch roll with the side kick. When you're comfortable, move around as you do it.

Punch Roll with Front Kick

A front kick can go higher than a drop kick, but puts you at greater risk of becoming unbalanced.

As you chop to change during the punch roll, grab both of your opponent's wrists—one in each hand. Deliver a front kick his/her mid-section. Be sure you're balanced and strong, so you can't be pushed over. Pull your opponent into your strike.

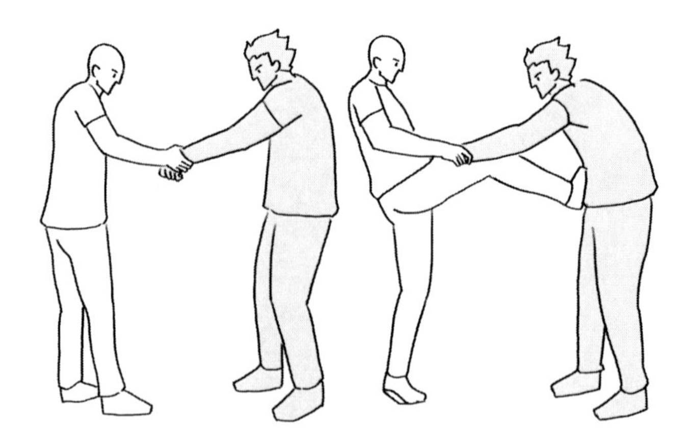

Exercise 68: Punch Roll with Front Kick

Practice the punch roll with the front kick. When you're comfortable, move around as you do it.

Exercise 69: Punch Roll with All Kicks

Put the three previous exercises together. You must use the right kick at the right time in the right place.

This is extremely good for improving your skills in distance and using the centerline principle. If your leg isn't in line, you'll miss, and if your distance is incorrect you'll be off-balance.

Practicing this exercise regularly will allow you to synchronize your hands and feet and know what to do with your body instinctively.

You don't have to grab both an opponent's wrists to do the front kick. Just do what works.

Add these kicks while you're practicing the Three Drills (lesson 32, exercise 62).

Related Chapters:

- Lesson 12: Centerline Principle
- Lesson 21: Punch Roll

LESSON 36: LEG GRAB

This lesson shows how you can grab hold of your opponent's leg if he/she tries to kick you above the waist.

As the kick comes in, move back and defend against it with Pak Sau. You need to move back to absorb the power, and you need to defend before grabbing; otherwise, you'll just be getting kicked in the ribs.

As soon as you perform Pak Sau, grab your opponent. Hook your elbow around his/her leg so it's held in tightly. Quickly reposition the hand you used for Pak Sau to protect your centerline in case your opponent punches.

Exercise 70: Leg Grab

Practice the leg grab.

Leg Grab Follow-Ups

Once you have a grip on your opponent's leg, a simple twist may be enough to put him/her off balance.

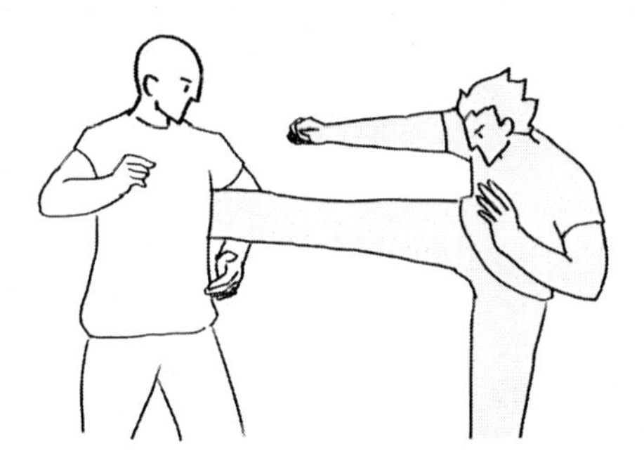

Exercise 71: Leg Grab with Twist

Do the leg grab and then try to unbalance your opponent with a twist.

Alternatively, you can drop an elbow onto your opponent's knee. Move your head with your elbow so your head isn't exposed.

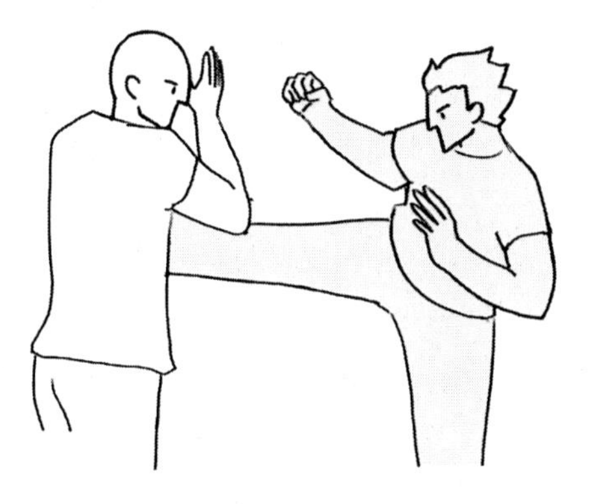

Keep your hand in place in case you need to defend.

Exercise 72: Leg Grab with Elbow

Do the leg grab with your elbow. Use the twist as well.

Related Chapters:

- Lesson 9: Grabbing
- Lesson 10: Pak Sau

LESSON 37: KICK COUNTERS

This lesson shows the three kicks used as counterattacks.

Stomp Kick Counter

Your opponent attacks with a straight punch. Use Pak Sau as a defense, then stomp kick his/her shin/knee

This kick counter happens very quickly after Pak Sau. The two are almost simultaneous.

It works because unless your opponent has a tremendous reach advantage, your kick will land first.

When you hit your opponent in the leg first, his/her punch will be stalled. The punch will be weakened and some damage will have been done to the leg. It will now be easier to take control, as opposed to rushing in at the start, when your chances of getting hit are much higher.

Exercise 73: Stomp Kick Counter

Have your partner throw some straight punches at you. Move around and defend against them. When you're ready, do a stomp kick.

Side Kick Counter

Your opponent attacks with a straight punch. Use Tan Sau as a defense, then do a side kick. You need to change the angle of your body to use the side kick.

If you are to the outside of your opponent's guard, then using Pak Sau to defend may be more convenient.

Exercise 74: Side Kick Counter

Have your partner throw some straight punches at you. Move around and defend against them. When you're ready, do a side kick.

Front Kick Counter

Defend against the straight punch, then deliver a front kick to your opponent's solar plexus.

Here it is from another angle. Notice that it may not be a straight front kick. It will depend on your position in relation to your opponent.

Exercise 75: Front Kick Counter

Have your partner throw some straight punches at you. Move around and defend against them. When you're ready, do a front kick.

If you know the one-two combination is coming, you can anticipate the second strike and use a front kick.

Exercise 76: One-Two Kick Counter

Have your partner throw one-two combinations at you. When the first punch comes in, use a stomp kick counter.

Use the same leg you did the stomp kick with to do a front kick as your partner throws the second punch.

Exercise 77: Random Kick Counters

Practice using the three kick counters in random order. The one you use depends on where you are in relation to your partner. If you're straight on, do a stomp kick. If you're to the side, use the side kick. If you want, use the front kick. If necessary, counter the one-two.

Related Chapters:

- Lesson 7: Tan Sau
- Lesson 8: Counterattack
- Lesson 10: Pak Sau
- Lesson 19: Three Kicks

LESSON 38: CHOP DRILL

This chop drill is another Wing Chun training drill used to enhance touch sensitivity, muscle memory, grabbing, distance, body awareness, centerline etc.

Your partner begins by chopping down at you. You chop to stop it.

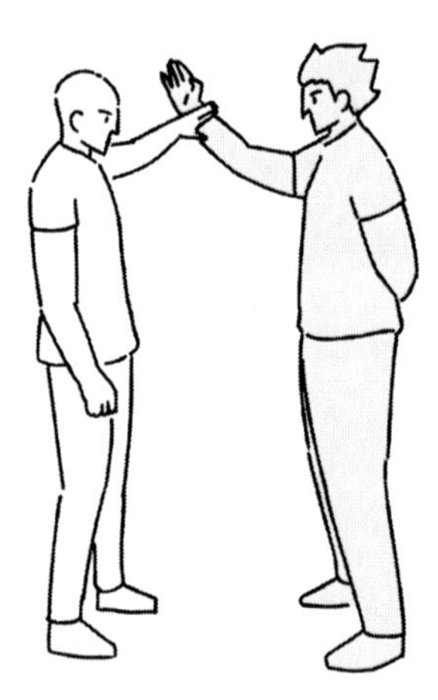

Your move your other hand underneath your opponent's arm to divert it, and then move your first hand over to pin his/her arm down at the elbow.

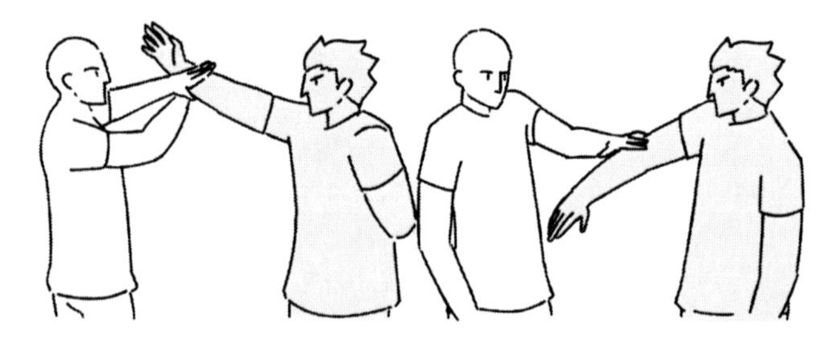

As you pin this arm down, use your other hand to chop down at him/her. Your partner defends in the same way you did and the drill continues.

Pinning at the elbow is very important. If you don't control your opponent's elbow in a real fight, then he/she will be able to break through and hit you.

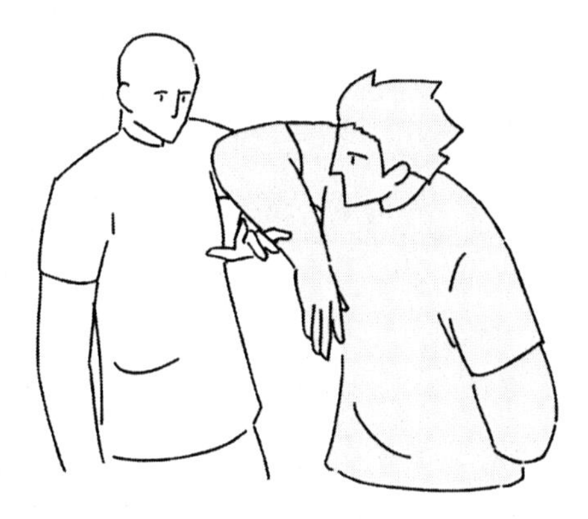

Exercise 78: Chop Drill

Practice the chop drill on both sides.

To change sides, use the same chop method as in the punch roll or the elbow drill. You can use the rhythm of chop, grab, and kick to change sides.

Chop Drill with Arm Lock

The following demonstrates how an arm lock can be applied during the chop drill. Defend against the initial chop and bring your hand underneath as usual, but this time keep hold of your opponent's arm. Twist it down and force your other hand onto his/her elbow.

Exercise 79: Chop Drill with Arm Lock

Practice the arm lock application of the chop drill.

Chop Drill with Knee

This demonstrates how a knee can be used during the chop drill. When you do the chop to change, bring your other hand underneath your opponent's, and then grab his/her arm. Make sure you control his/her elbow.

Throw a quick knee into his/her thigh or midsection.

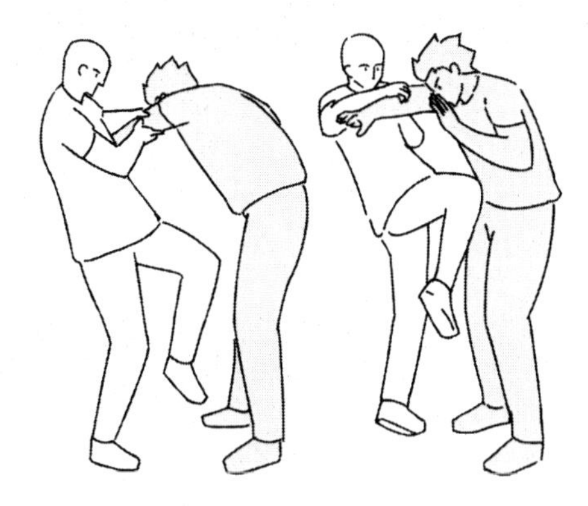

Exercise 80: Chop Drill with Knee

Practice the chop drill and apply a knee.

Exercise 81: Random Chop Drill

Practice the chop drill and use a random attack every now and again.

Related Chapters:

- Lesson 9: Grabbing
- Lesson 16: The Chop
- Lesson 21: Punch Roll
- Lesson 29: Elbow Drill

LESSON 39: GRAB AND ATTACK

This lesson focuses on deflecting a strike and grabbing your opponent's striking arm in one motion, while simultaneously attacking. You have to have good reflexes to do this. It's where all the drills pay off.

Grab and Punch

This lesson teaches the basic grab-and-punch movement, as well as the importance of maintaining distance.

As your opponent throws a straight punch, deflect it on the outside of your arm and grab him/her by the lower arm. This is the same type of grab as in exercise 40 (three kicks application) but now you will go faster. As soon as you grab his/her arm, step forward and pull your opponent into your attack.

Your attacking arm must be firm on his/her upper arm; otherwise, he/she can elbow you.

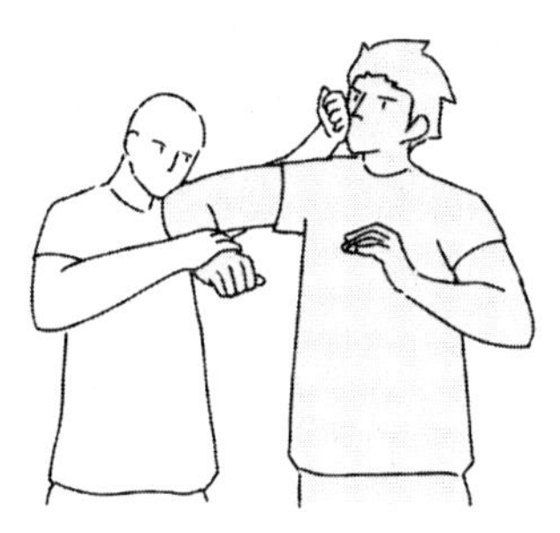

It's best to be cautious about your distance. If you're far away, you can always pull your opponent in, but if you're too close, he/she can hurt you.

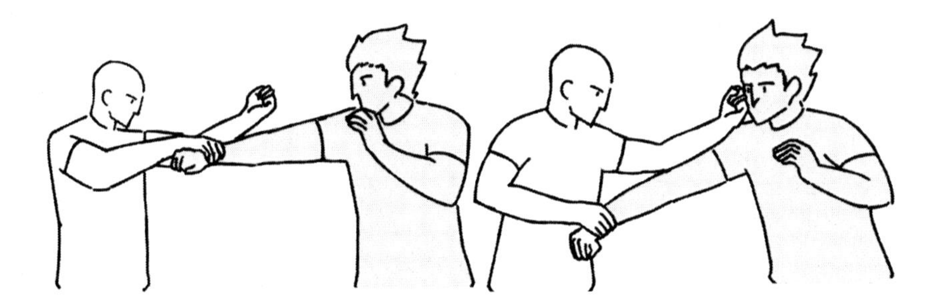

Move with your opponent to maintain correct distance. If your opponent forces you back, step back. If he/she steps back, step forward.

Exercise 82: Grab and Punch

Practice doing the grab and punch as a single, fluid movement.

Grab and Rib Punch

This shows the grab and punch in a different target area, the ribs. It takes advantage of your opponent's forward movement.

As your opponent punches, grab his/her arm and move in to punch his/her ribs. Your punch should land as he/she moves in.

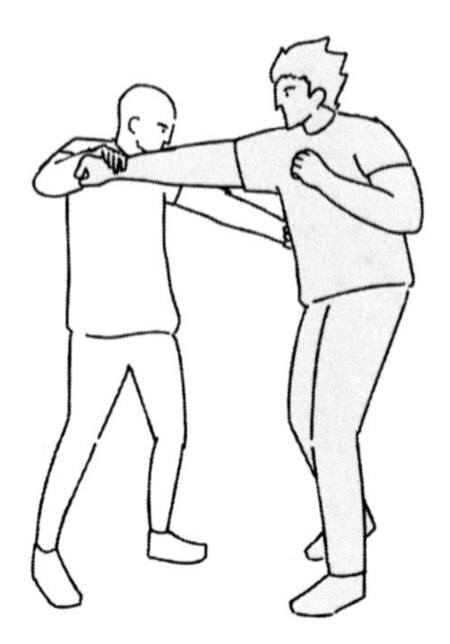

Alternate sides as you do it.

Ensure you hold your opponent's hand up to protect your head. Be aware that he/she may drag it down. You want your opponent's body in line with yours, but his/her hand out of the way.

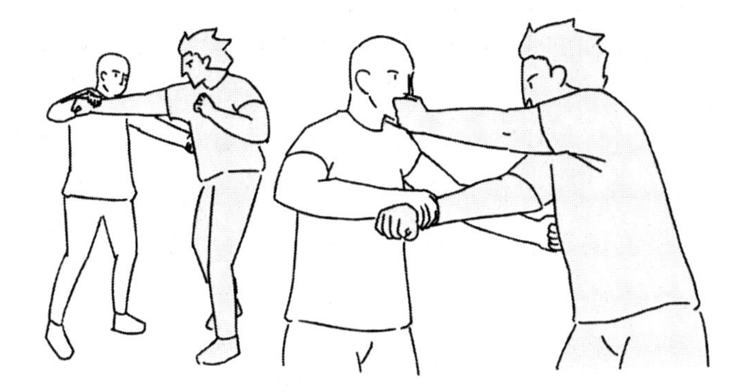

Be conscious of your distance. If you're too far, you won't be able to hit him/her, and if you're too close, your opponent will be able to bend his/her arm and elbow you.

Exercise 83: Grab and Rib Punch

Practice doing the grab and rib punch in one fluid motion.

Grab with Stomp Kick

This demonstrates the grab with the stomp kick, and re-emphasizes the importance of balance.

As the punch comes in, grab and kick your opponent in the knee (go for the shin in training).

It's important that you grab your opponent and are in control before you kick; otherwise, it will be easy for him/her to upset your balance.

Pull your opponent's arm and push out your kick at the same time. If your leg isn't strong enough, your opponent can push you over. This is where the half squats pay off.

Step back and do the same thing on the other side.

Exercise 84: Grab with Stomp Kick

Practice the grab with stomp kick exercise on both sides.

Grab with Side Kick

This demonstrates how to do a grab with a side kick and re-emphasizes the importance of distance.

As the punch comes in, use Pak Sau and then grab your opponent's arm. Give him/her a side kick to the knee or just above it.

Step back and do the same on the other side.

You should have enough distance that your opponent's arm can't reach you. Even if you don't use your hands, you should be okay.

Have a slight forward lean. If you lean back, your opponent can push you over. If you're leaning forward, then even if your opponent steps back, you can maintain the right distance for an attack.

Never straighten your leg completely. If your leg is completely straight and your opponent moves back even a little, you'll miss.

If you aim for your leg to still be a little bent on landing, then you can still get your opponent if he/she steps back. If your opponent doesn't step back, then your strike will do more damage.

Exercise 85: Grab with Side Kick

Practice the grab with side kick on both sides.

When moving naturally, you have to be fast. Grab and attack straight away; otherwise, your opponent won't be there.

Double Side Kick

This shows how to repeat the side kick. It's important to understand where both your and your opponent's bodies are, and where to place your leg.

As your opponent's punch comes in, grab his/her arm and deliver a side kick to his/her midsection.

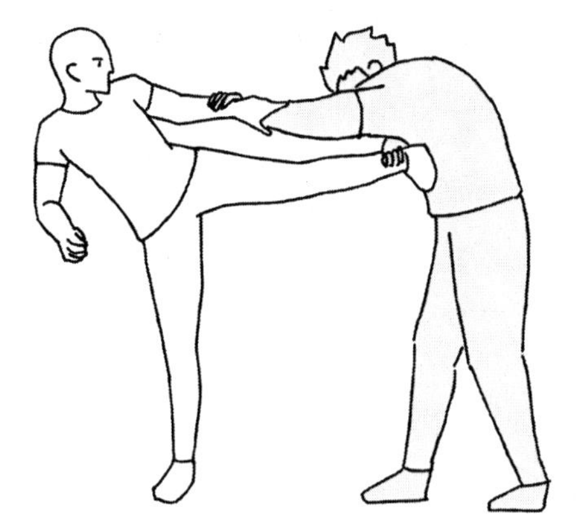

Bring your foot back down to the ground and then kick him/her again.

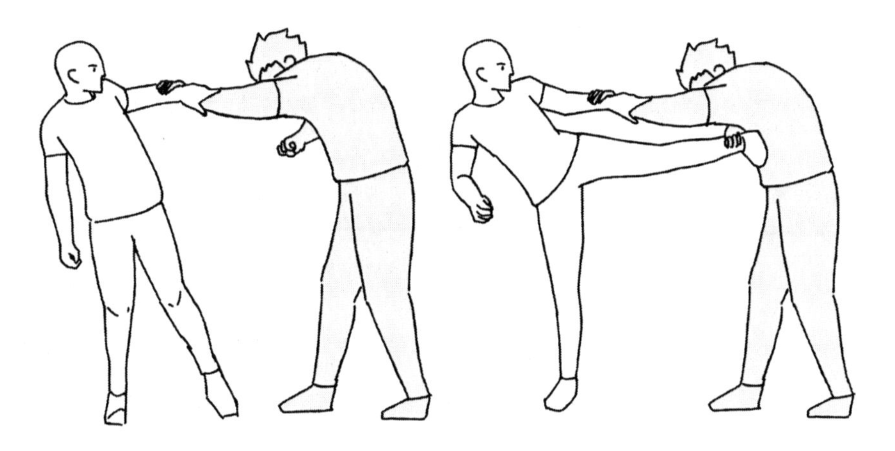

Exercise 86: Double Side Kick

Practice the double side kick.

The kicks do not need to go to your opponent's midsection, or even to the same target. You could kick low to your opponent's knee first and then higher into his/her midsection, for example.

Grab and Elbow

This lesson demonstrates how to use your elbow with a grab. Elbows can do a lot of damage, but you need to be up close and inside your opponent's guard, which results in a greater risk of you being hit.

Deflect your opponent's punch and grab his/her arm. Bring your elbow up so it's parallel to the ground.

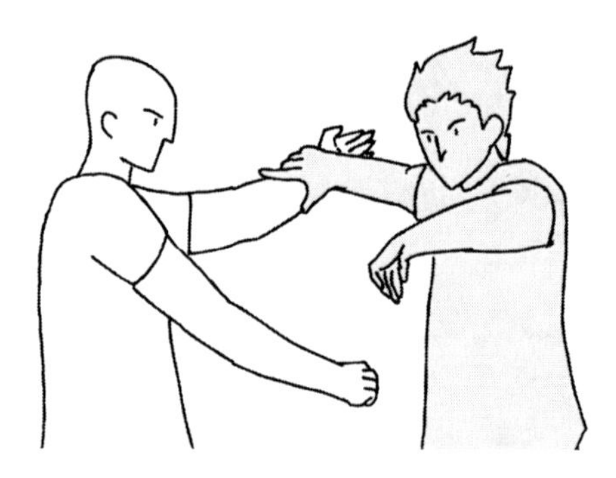

Step forward and drive your elbow into your opponent's chest or head. It's best to keep the strike around the same height as your shoulder. If your opponent is too tall, don't aim for his/her head.

The movement should be fluid and fast.

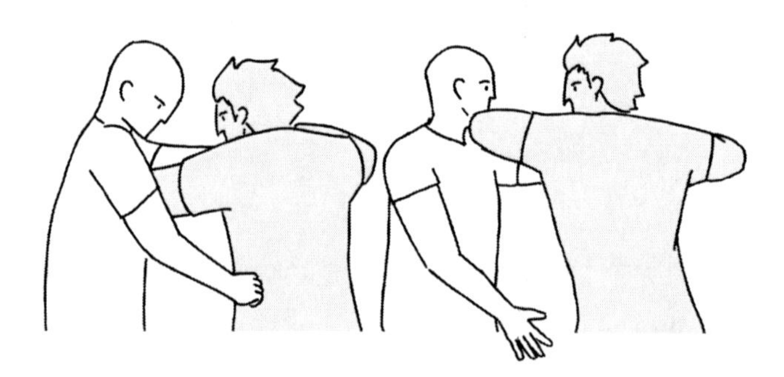

Exercise 87: Grab and Elbow

Practice the grab and elbow.

As a variation, when you bring your elbow up, angle it so it's higher than your hand.

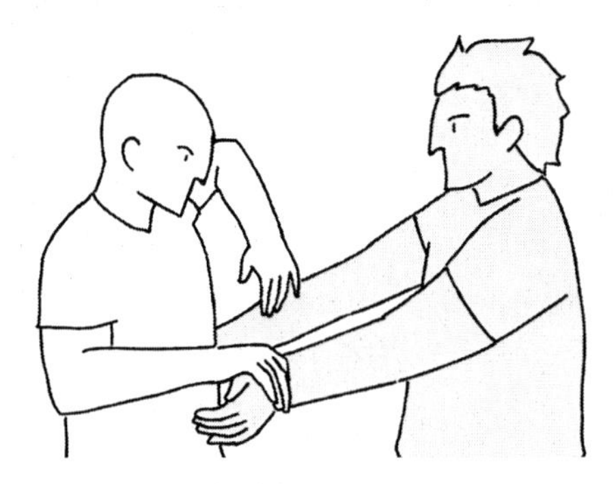

Crash down onto your target. Do not lean forward. Step in so your whole body creates the power while you stay balanced and in control.

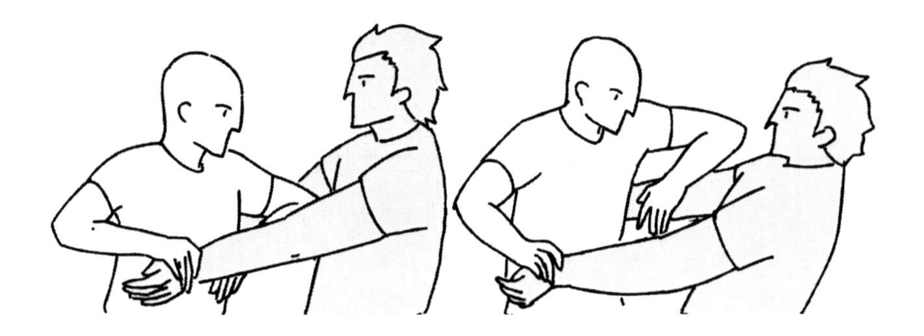

Exercise 88: Grab and Elbow Variation

Practice this variation of the grab and elbow.

Grab and Knee

This shows you how to use a grab with your knee. Like elbows, knees can do a lot of damage but you need to be up close and inside your opponent's guard, resulting in a greater risk of you being hit.

As your opponent strikes, deflect and grab his/her arm at the elbow with both hands. You must control his/her elbow, or you'll be at risk of getting hit in the face.

Put a knee into his/her thigh, groin (not in training), or higher if you want.

Do not use a big movement. Make it small and sharp.

Exercise 89: Grab and Knee

Practice the grab and knee.

Exercise 90: Grab and Counter

Have your partner throw straight attacks as you. Grab and counter in any way you wish.

Related Chapters:

- Lesson 1: The Half Squat
- Lesson 10: Pak Sau
- Lesson 19: Three Kicks

LESSON 40: DOUBLE GRABS

This lesson builds on grab techniques with double grabs. Repetitive training in things such as the three drills make your reflexes and muscle memory very fast. These double-grab exercises demonstrate how training pays off in more realistic fighting scenarios.

In a real fight, you won't know what your opponent will do or how he/she will react to your movements, but it won't matter. The training conditions your body to react. No matter what your opponent does, you'll be able to defend and attack with Wing Chun techniques.

Basic Double Grab

As your opponent punches, deflect the punch with Tan Sau, then move your other hand over to pin his/her arm down.

As you pin his/her arm, punch. Your opponent defends with Tan Sau or by chopping your arm.

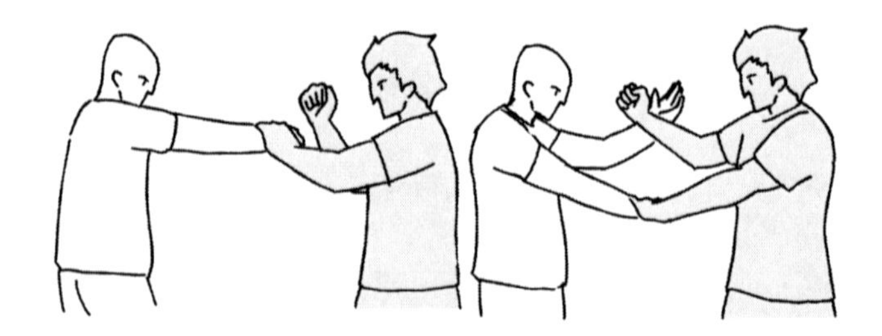

Grab this arm and punch him/her in the solar plexus.

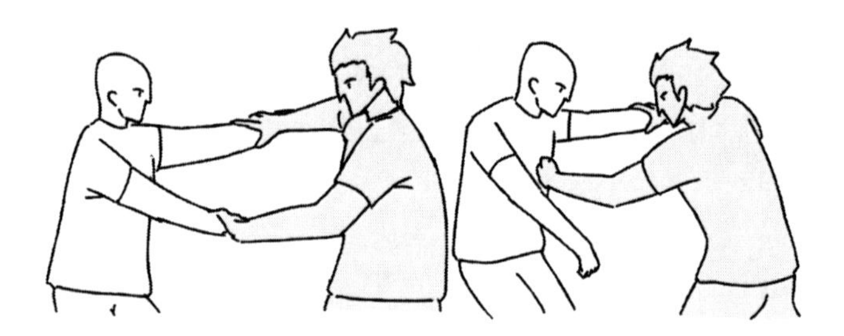

Exercise 91: Basic Double Grab

Practice the basic double grab on both sides of your body.

Bong Sau Double Grab

This combines Bong Sau with the double grab.

As your opponent's punch comes in, deflect it with Bong Sau. Bring your other hand up to grab his/her wrist.

Bring your Bong Sau hand up to strike your opponent in the face. Lock your arm into his/hers so you can't be pushed.

Your opponent uses his/her other hand to defend against your strike.

Grab this hand and turn your opponent to expose his/her side. Punch him/her straight in the ribs. Do not retract your arm before punching. Shift your weight and punch with your whole body, as you did in the grab and rib punch exercise.

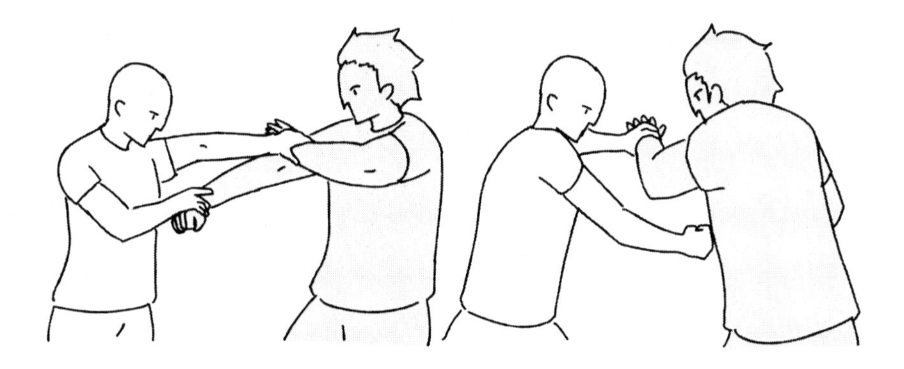

Exercise 92: Bong Sau Double Grab

Practice the Bong Sau double grab.

Advanced Double Grab

This is another double grab exercise.

As your opponent punches, defend with Tan Sau.

He/she throws a second punch. Very quickly bring your free hand over to pin his/her original punching hand, while your other hand defends against this new punch.

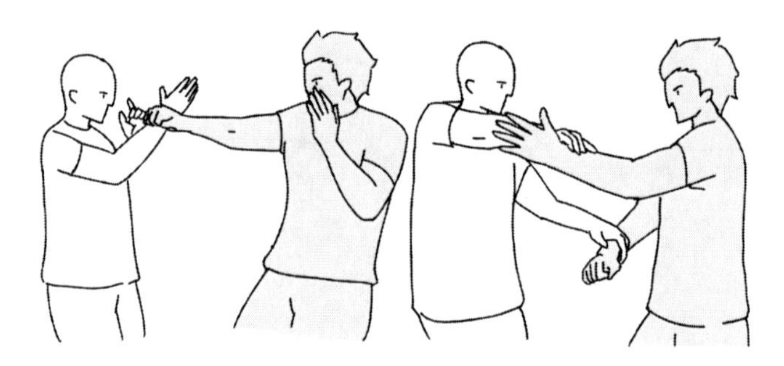

Grab his/her current punching hand and use your other hand to punch as you pull him/her in.

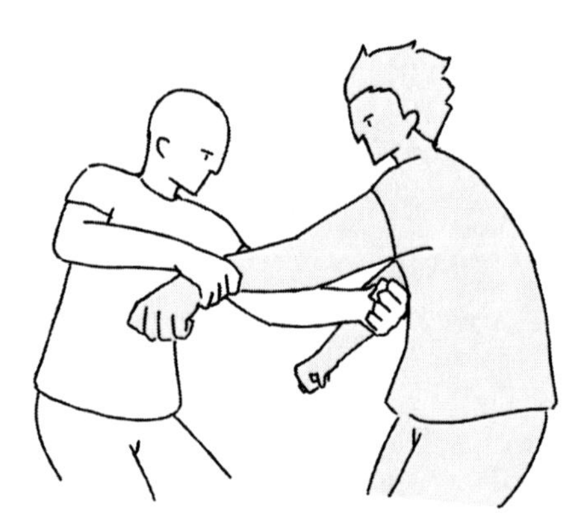

Move your punching hand over to grab your opponent's arm. Turn your opponent to expose his/her side, and attack his/her ribs.

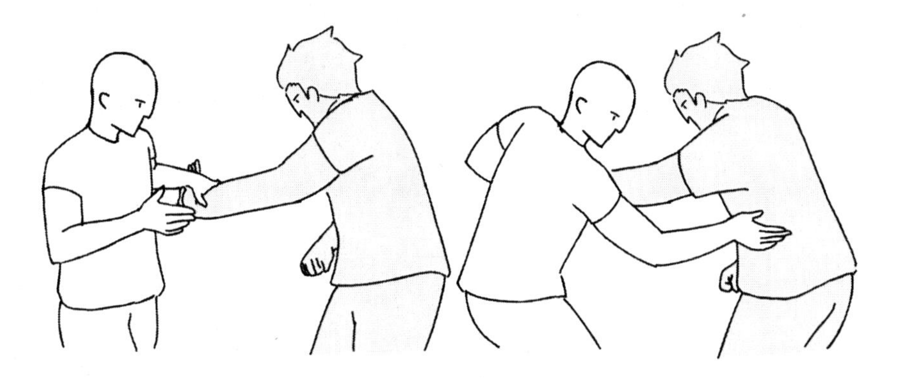

Exercise 93: Advanced Double Grab

Practice the advanced double grab.

Advanced Double Grab 2

This exercise is yet another double grab, but it focuses more on the use of very fast movements to distract and confuse your opponent, which creates openings for attack.

Your opponent strikes and you defend with Pak Sau.

Move your other hand over to pin down this punching hand. Strikes at your opponent with the hand you used to do Pak Sau. As expected, your opponent defends.

Bring your non-striking hand underneath your opponent's and grabs his/her defending hand. Pull his/her arm over so it blocks his/her other arm from defending.

As you pull your opponent's arm, strike at his/her face.

Exercise 94: Advanced Double Grab 2

Practice the advanced double grab 2.

Double Grab and Chop

This double grab exercise makes use of the chop.

As your opponent, punches use Tan Sau to defend. Bring your other hand over to pin his/her arm down.

As you pin his/her arm down, punch. Your opponent defends with Pak Sau.

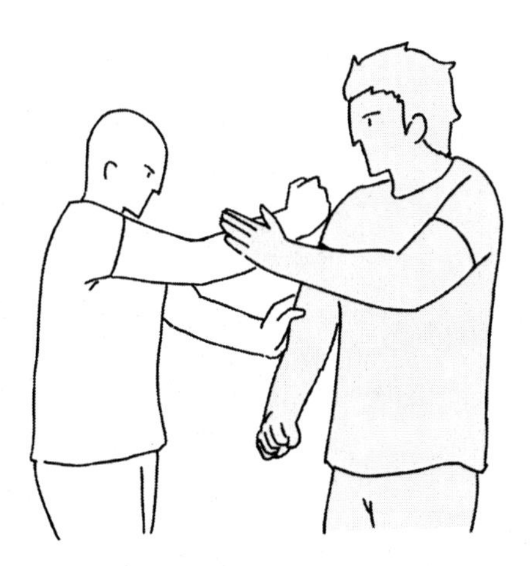

Bring your other hand over to pin his/her arm. Swap the positions of your hands instantly and deliver a chop to your opponent's throat.

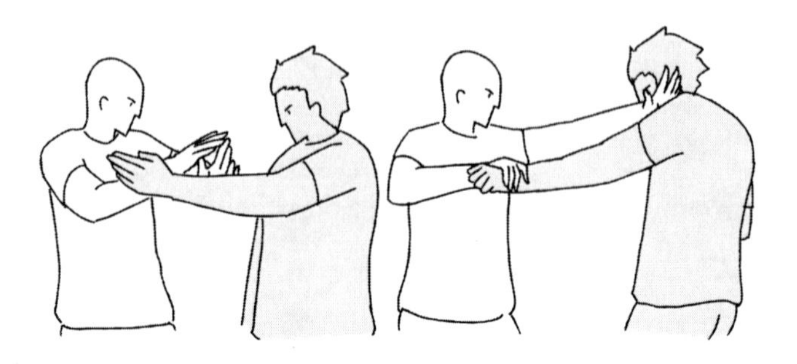

Exercise 95: Double Grab and Chop

Practice the double grab and chop.

Related Chapters:

- Lesson 7: Tan Sau
- Lesson 10: Pak Sau
- Lesson 13: Bong Sau
- Lesson 16: The Chop

LESSON 41: TACKLE DEFENSE

This lesson shows how you can defend against someone trying to tackle you. Wing Chun is primarily a non-ground-fighting martial art.

To learn more about ground fighting, please visit:

www.SurvivalFitnessPlan.com/Ground-Fighting-Techniques

Your opponent moves in to tackle you. Widen your legs and drop your center of gravity to ensure a stable base; otherwise, you'll end up on the floor. You have to do this as soon as your opponent comes in.

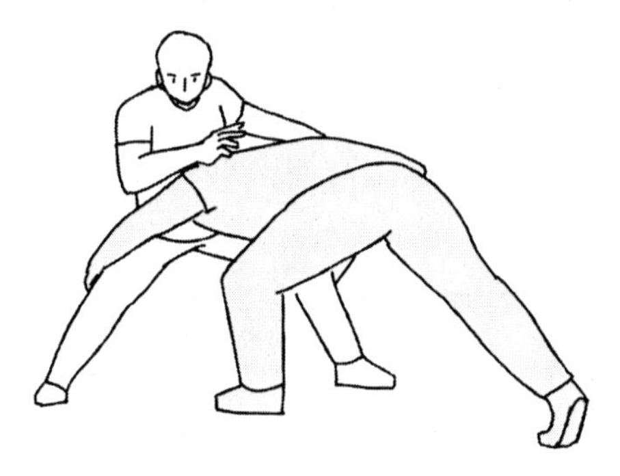

Put your weight on top of your opponent to force him/her down. This will make it hard for him/her to push you back. If you want, you can put your elbow into his/her back as you drop down (not in training).

Your arm goes around your opponent's neck. This picture shows the move from the opposite side, so you can see. Hold his/her neck tightly.

Strike your opponent. For example, punch his/her ribs, punch his/her leg, and/or drive your elbow into his/her arm.

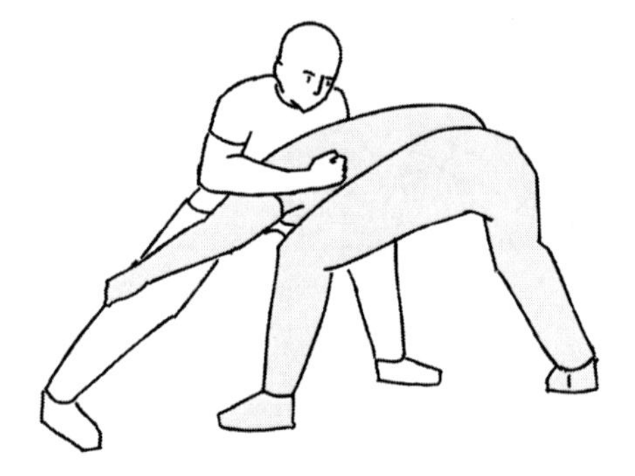

Grab your opponent's leg at the knee and push to force him/her over.

Exercise 96: Tackle Defense

Practice this defense against the tackle.

If your opponent grabs you so your arms are pinned, you can force your forehead into the side of his/her face. Do not hit your forehead into the top of your opponent's head, or you'll get hurt as well.

LESSON 42: SPARRING

To spar is to fight against one or more partners for training purposes. Conditional variations are limited only to your imagination. Hands only, feet only, eyes closed—anything goes.

Start slowly. As your skills improve, you can increase your speed. As your fitness increases, you can do more timed rounds.

Only go as hard/fast as the least experienced fighter can safely go. This may be dictated by the more experienced fighter if he/she feels that his/her sparring partner is going harder/faster than he/she can safely control.

Note: Your power level is separate from your aggressiveness level. You can still be at 100% aggressiveness while only using 20% power.

Protective equipment is highly recommended.

Tapping Out

Tapping out is something you can do when you submit/give up, such as when a lock starts to hurt. Tap your training partner at least twice so that he/she feels it. Your partner must disengage immediately. If you cannot reach your opponent, then tap the floor. A verbal tap-out, like "stop," can also be used.

Exercise 97: Sparring

Include timed sparring rounds in your training.

THANKS FOR READING

Dear reader,

Thank you for reading *Basic Wing Chun Training.*

If you enjoyed this book, please leave a review where you bought it. It helps more than most people think.

Don't forget your FREE book chapters!

You will also be among the first to know of FREE review copies, discount offers, bonus content, and more.

Go to:

https://offers.SFNonfictionBooks.com/Free-Chapters

Thanks again for your support.

REFERENCES

Cheung, W. (1852). *Dynamic Chi Sao by William Cheung.* Unique Publications.

DeMile, J. (1977). *Tao of Wing Chun Do, Vol. 2: Bruce Lee's Chi Sao*. Tao of Wing Chun Do.

Gutierrez, V. (2009). *WingTsun. Chi Sao II.* Sportimex.

Yimm Lee, J. (1972). *Wing Chun Kung-Fu.* Ohara Publications.

AUTHOR RECOMMENDATIONS

Discover How to Do Wing Chun Chi Sao

You'll love this manual, because it will teach you how to adapt Chi Sao to real fighting scenarios.

Get it now.

www.SFNonfictionBooks.com/Chi-Sao

EVADING &
ESCAPING
URBAN ESCAPE AND EVASION TECHNIQUES FOR CIVILIANS

ABOUT SAM FURY

Sam Fury has had a passion for survival, evasion, resistance, and escape (SERE) training since he was a young boy growing up in Australia.

This led him to years of training and career experience in related subjects, including martial arts, military training, survival skills, outdoor sports, and sustainable living.

These days, Sam spends his time refining existing skills, gaining new skills, and sharing what he learns via the Survival Fitness Plan website.

www.SurvivalFitnessPlan.com

amazon.com/author/samfury
goodreads.com/SamFury
facebook.com/AuthorSamFury
instagram.com/AuthorSamFury
youtube.com/SurvivalFitnessPlan

Made in United States
North Haven, CT
21 April 2024